PRIESTLY CELIBACY AND MATURITY

PRIESTLY CELIBACY AND MATURITY

DAVID P. O'NEILL

SHEED AND WARD : NEW YORK

CONTENTS

PRIESTLY CELIBACY AND MATURITY

I:

SOMEONE MUST BEGIN

THE CELIBACY RULE of Roman Catholic priests is under discussion today as never before in the history of the Church. The decision of the Second Vatican Council to restore the order of the diaconate as a functioning part of the ministry, and to allow married men to become deacons, has sparked a wide-ranging public discussion on the whole question of a celibate clergy and its relevance in the modern world. A whole trend of thinking on the psychology of the priest and his changing role in Western society has prepared the way for this public debate.

This book aims to look at the reasons for celibacy from the viewpoint of the priest, to explain the idealism of Christian dedication that should inspire it, and to look honestly at the difficulties that have lent weight to proposals for renewal and reform. It may seem to some rather strange for a priest to enter into such open discussion at this stage. However, I have been a Catholic priest, living in dedicated celibacy these twenty-five years, and it seems to me that I have earned the right to speak; it has been on my mind for a long time that some priest should write on the inner form and dedication of our life as priests. My reasons for doing so will become more clear as this book proceeds. There have never been lacking any number of critics from outside the Church to pose very seriously the question as to whether it is a good thing for priests to be bound to stay unmarried. However, from the priest's own viewpoint, very little has so far appeared in English. Perhaps it is because this discussion has been slowly taking shape in the minds of many priests and is limited so far to the quiet talk of rectories, and perhaps, because priests of writing talent are busy about less controversial subjects. It still seems odd to me that it should be left to a priest from the faraway places of the South Pacific to make a beginning with a book of this type.

I feel that it is a matter of great importance to begin to speak clearly on this issue. I feel, too, that the danger of shocking many Catholic people, and some priests, is something that must be undertaken in the name of honesty and truth, for the sake of all that is to be gained for the life of the Church and her priests by open discussion. After all, this is the same kind of uneasy shock that came over many people at the thought of having the prayers of the Mass in English instead of Latin, at the thought of the Church making a humble and penitent approach towards unity with the churches of the Reformation tradition. Where such a shock is truly a yielding to honesty, truth, and charity, it is the beginning of a good step forward.

During the years that I have been a priest, I have known, intimately and casually, many hundreds of priests in my own country, New Zealand. While most of them, like myself, have been natives of this country, large numbers have come here from Ireland, England, the United States, Australia, Holland and other places. I have spent a good deal of time visiting with priests in Australia, England, Ireland, and the United States, and have been interested to find that the common elements of our priesthood have produced, in these countries of like social structure and heritage, a way of living for priests that is so very similar. What I have to say, then, about the priests of the Western Church is based on a wide enough experience of priests in the English-speaking areas. What I know of the ways of priests in the other areas of the Western Church has been gathered from conversation with priests from these places, and from reading. In the kind of book this is going to be, my knowledge and experience of priestly life should be sufficient. While it is certainly something of a disadvantage to live on an island in the ocean at the end of the world, it also brings an element of detachment from traditions and customs which can be a burden as often as a support. It is because we are so far away from the old centers of Church tradition in Europe and the United States that we feel the challenge to make our voices heard as detached observers.

In spite of the fairly wide experience of priestly life and ways which I am able to draw upon, my conclusions in this book will still be very far from final. The thing that needs to be done at this stage, in my opinion, is to open the question of priestly celibacy for mature discussion and rational debate. In order to do this, we shall find it necessary to look at the history of celibacy among the priests of the West, at the idealism that can inspire it in the light of modern theology and psychology, and at the problems which it presents to the life of priests of the present day. In developing some positive suggestions for a renewal of the idealism of celibacy for secular priests we will be led to examine critically the whole scheme of training of deacons and priests. It will become apparent that unless the serious deficiencies in the present type of formation of young men for the Church's ministry are remedied, the prospect of celibacy becoming a more meaningful form of personal dedication of mature men will be negligible. We will see that the young man who offers himself to the Church must be guided into mature manhood before the dedication of celibacy can bear the full fruit of Christian love and service.

There are many people in the Church today who feel that she should preserve carefully her rather monolithic image of confident agreement on everything, an image that Catholics, and especially priests, have no serious differences of opinion in matters of religion. People who think this way find deep security in the thought that the Church has all the answers to the problems of religion and even to all the problems of the modern world; they feel strongly that public discussion and controversy have no place in the inner life of the Church. They consider that the Church, the guardian of truth and the center of Christian life, should show to the world a shining image of truth, beauty, and charity in such a way that all human differences are hidden quietly away. While there can be a place for discreet controversy in the learned periodicals of the clergy, especially those written in Latin, these controversies should not be allowed to disturb the minds of lay people, much less interest the minds of those who are only too ready to treat the Catholic Church as an enemy of humanity.

This view, if it ever had any reality-value, certainly has none today. The example alone of the inner workings of the Second Vatican Council, so fully publicized throughout the world, indicates that the Church of today has deliberately opened its heart to the world. It has opened its mind so that the world can see not only its central core of revealed truth, but also the difficulties we find in choosing human forms in which to clothe the things that are divine. We must struggle to find human words, and human forms of social structure and institution, to turn the truth into a relevant and well-understood message, and to give corporate human form to the divine mystery which St. Paul described as the Body of Christ.

In any case, even if the Council had never happened, it would still be true that our image must be an objective and real one. There is no room in the world of today for a mythical Church. We are, after all, the extension of the Incarnation into human society. As the Second Person of the Trinity, coming into the world, entered fully into the human situation by becoming a real man, not just a shining image of a man, so his Church is a body of real men and women. These are men and women who live indeed in the light of Christ and in the energizing love of the Spirit, but they remain real people. They have to strive with all their being towards the holiness of the Father, to stretch their minds to understand more and more deeply the message he has given to them in Christ. They must, too, use all the ordinary laborious means of discussion, argument and controversy, all that they can know of man, his present ways and thought-forms, to find suitable expressions in each succeeding age for the social structure and organization with which to clothe the living body of Christ incarnate in the men of today.

To treat the celibacy of the Catholic priest as I would wish to do, I would need to be expert in the fields of the social history of the West, of psychology, sociology, theology and scripture. While I have some acquaintance with these fields of study, I must leave myself open, in all of them, to the judgment of men more learned than I. However, I do have the experience of my own years of life in the priesthood, and I have known and listened to hundreds of other priests; perhaps it is best that some rather ordinary priest like myself should make this beginning. If, in doing so, I give offense to any, within the Church or out of it, I beg their kindly pardon in advance, and assure them that my mind is as open as I would wish theirs to be, on this subject as on any other.

For this book does not aim to be an authoritative work. Neither does it aim to be scholarly in the usual sense. So many fields of scholarship have been drawn on in writing it that I can only hope to have fairly interpreted the view of the real scholars from whom I have learned by word and writing. There is no pretense, either, that this book is scientifically objective. Its subject matter does not lend itself easily to the method of scientific investigation; in those areas where methods of social research might apply, the basic work has not, to my knowledge, so far been carried out.

I have not tried to write a psychological treatise on the priesthood, but rather to make use of some general conclusions of psychology to illustrate the subject of celibacy and the life-conditions of the priest. Wherever possible, therefore, I have avoided both the technical language of the psychology schools and the taking of a positive stand in the theoretical disputes of this discipline. I have made use of the basic concepts and simpler terminology of many leading psychologists, according as their insight seems best to shed light on the particular problem of the priestly life under discussion.

Nor is this a book of philosophy; I have not adopted as my own the framework of any philosophical school. Inevitably I will be ranging into the fields of ontology and cosmology, and, again, will express myself in the thought that seems most appropriate at the moment. If some learned reader tells me that my thought owes more to Augustine than to Thomas, that my life-view suggests the influence of Kierkegaard and Heidegger rather than that of Maritain, I may well be impressed, perhaps mystified, but not concerned. Having stated that I am not attempting to provide a scholarly textbook, nor a work of scientific social research, nor a psychology of the priest, nor a work of philosophy, it remains to say what I am really trying to do.

I aim to say something definite and concrete about the celibacy of the Catholic priest from the viewpoint of one who is a priest himself. I shall use my own life-experience of celibacy and the experience I have shared with so many other priests, to make a positive and critical examination of the life of the priest of today. I shall develop, from the pages of history and from some modern commentaries, what I consider to be the present meaning of celibacy in the life of priests. This present meaning, celibacy-as-experienced, will be measured against the ideals which we shall see from scriptural theology and from personal and social psychology. From examining some sociological trends we may see something of the priest's role in the future of our society and the part celibacy should play in the formation of this role. As we progress I shall be making some practical suggestions for a renewal of celibacy. I shall be suggesting the practical arrangements and conditions for the life of the priest, which will serve to promote the ideals, both theological and psychological, which we shall discuss. This will involve a discussion of the education, training, and pastoral formation of priests, as well as a consideration of many aspects of their working life.

Those who are seeking in this book an argument for the abolition of celibacy will be disappointed. It will be evident from what I have said already that I consider that the dedication of celibacy should play a greater rather than a lesser part in the life and outlook of the priest. Insofar as this book has a thesis, an argument, this is it. I will be attempting to emphasize this thesis from what I am and what I experience, from the sharing of life in the priesthood, and from whatever insight I can express from my knowledge of the various thought-systems which I have just mentioned.

My approach, therefore, must be rather subjective. There are solidly objective elements in the widely-recognized facts of the situation, in the conclusions of many fields of learning, in the quotations from many writers. However, the synthesis is personal to me—it is the way I look at it after twenty-five years of living it. Because it is this kind of book, who I am and what I am has some importance. It may save publisher and reviewers some trouble if I repeat that I am an ordinary kind of secular priest with a fairly normal range of pastoral experience. I am not, as are some writers on the modern Church, another person in disguise.

Like most other secular priests I was a parish assistant for some years, before becoming pastor of a city parish. Along the way I found myself more and more in the field of social welfare and casework, and was asked to organize a Catholic Charities service for the diocese. This has given me a more than usual number of friends who are alcoholics, murderers, unmarried mothers, psychologists, thieves, social workers, drug addicts, magistrates, adopted children, policemen, and juvenile delinquents. Maybe this gives me some claim to be able to understand priests. It certainly gives me a habit of trying to look to the roots of a human situation and to be honest and realistic in assessing its possibilities. I have tried to be candid in expressing my own views on the celibacy of priests—I felt that otherwise this book would not be worth writing. I have tried to be fair in considering the views of all the important people who disagree with me—otherwise, maybe, this book would not be worth reading.

The one deep conviction I have is that the time is overdue for an open discussion of the forms that the priesthood of the Western Church must take to meet and speak to the men of the next fifty or a hundred years. While no quick changes in our present custom of celibacy for priests are likely or desirable, it is only by slow and careful discussion among open-minded people that such changes as I will suggest can be tested and evaluated.

I shall be pointing to many frustrations and anxieties which I know are in the minds of many priests and many of the lay people of the Church. I am experienced enough in counseling those suffering from anxiety and frustration to know that open discussion and the revealing of inner feelings are part of the way to health and security. Self-knowledge, self-assessment, self-examination, are essential for human growth and maturity. As well as knowing God, so one of the old philosophers tells us, we must also know ourselves; within the Church, we must not only know the truth of the divine message and the way in which God shows himself to man, but we must learn to know ourselves far more deeply and to know the human institutions which go to make up the incarnation of the Church in any present age. This is the way of maturity and true development within the Church, the way towards the inner holiness of love which is the gift of the Spirit.

2:

HOW IT CAME ABOUT

So ENMESHED do we become in the social forms which surround us, that it is quite difficult for most Catholics, lay and clergy, to realize that there is no essential connection between the Catholic priesthood and celibacy. They find it quite a difficulty when they are told that at all periods in the history of the Church there have been married men with wives and families who were also Catholic priests in full communion with the Pope in Rome. Not only have these married priests had this full communion with the rest of the Church, but they have had official and oft-repeated approval of their custom.

This approval of a married priesthood within the structure of the Church has been restated by modern Popes, as, for example, by Pope Pius XI in his encyclical on the Catholic priesthood some thirty years ago (*Ad Catholici Sacerdotii*). After a long discussion of the obligation of celibacy for the priests of the West and of the good reasons for preserving this, he goes on to state very clearly his approval for the opposite custom existing in the Catholic Churches of the Eastern tradition:

> We do not wish that what we have said in commendation of clerical celibacy should be interpreted as though it were our mind in any way to blame or, as it were, disapprove of the different discipline legitimately prevailing in the Oriental Church.

The continuing custom, followed by the last three Popes, of granting permission for ordination to the Catholic priesthood of married men who were formerly ministers of another church, gives a clear indication that even in the Church of the West the connection between celibacy and priesthood is clearly seen to be not in any way essential, but rather customary and legal.

Historians give us no clear picture of the origin of this custom. We do know that there was no sign in the life of Jesus and his apostles that they saw any essential connection between the priesthood and celibacy. We know that in apostolic times married priests were common. It is this early tradition which has persisted through to our own day, with the Church's full approval, in the Catholic Churches of the East, and in the Orthodox churches; all of these Churches are very conscious of preserving their ancient apostolic traditions.

These early traditions were emphasized at the Ecumenical Council of Nicaea, in 325. Socrates, a historian writing at about the end of the same century, describes how some bishops, during the Council,

undertook to propose a new law. They intended to forbid married bishops, priests and deacons to have conjugal relations with their wives after ordination. Paphnutius, a venerable bishop from Upper Egypt, who himself had always been a celibate, observed that it would be very imprudent to impose such a burden of continence not only on clerics, but also on their wives, and that it would be enough to abide by the ancient tradition of the Church and forbid clerics to marry after ordination . . . his authority carried the day.[1]

Another Eastern Council a little later in the same century, held at Gangres, was concerned to uphold the holiness of Christian marriage; this Council issued a formal condemna-

[1] Socrates, *Hist. Eccles.* I, 2, quoted in Poulet-Raemers' *Church History,* St. Louis: B. Herder Book Co., 1934, p. 142.

tion against anyone who "draws a distinction between a married and an unmarried priest, and says that it is not fitting to share in the oblation made by the former."[2]

In the West, there is no record of a law of celibacy for priests during the first three hundred years of the Church's life. Early in the fourth century, a local Council at Elvira in Spain, and, a little later, other Councils, passed laws imposing celibacy as an obligation on priests. These Councils formed into law what had probably been an increasing custom in many parts of the Church. By this time it was already established in the East that while married men could be ordained as priests, once a man was ordained he could not then enter into marriage.

We find many Western Councils repeating over and over again the new law of celibacy, not only for priests but also for deacons and subdeacons, and even sometimes forbidding those already married to have intercourse with their wives. The frequency with which this matter comes up for repeated legislation in local Synods and Councils through to the late Middle Ages indicates that the enforcement of this law was an issue of long-standing difficulty. A generous documentation of celibacy legislation in the early Middle Ages, with candid contemporary comments on the life of the clergy, is available in Henry C. Lea's *History of Sacerdotal Celibacy in the Christian Church*. Written one hundred years ago, with an anti-Catholic bias typical of the time, it still provides a wealth of documented material. Lea's general conclusions are confirmed, as we shall see, by the more sober historians of the present day.[3]

During the ninth, tenth, and eleventh centuries, a time during which we have increasing evidence from the his-

---

[2] Cf. *Ibid.*

[3] Henry C. Lea, *History of Sacerdotal Celibacy in the Christian Church*, New York: Russell & Russell, Inc.

torians, it is clear that there was among the clergy of the West a fairly widespread disregard of the celibacy law, a disregard often openly recognized in the phrasing of local Synods. This is well described by Bernard Guillemain, a present-day historian:

Clerical incontinence, in the moral degradation to which the clergy had sunk, principally took the form of a dissolute sexual life and the keeping of concubines. Shameful examples abounded, and the elder Anselm of Lucca, later Alexander II, asserted that 'all the priests and levites have wives.' The virtues necessary to the priestly ministry had fallen into such oblivion that . . . others felt it necessary for a woman to keep house for a priest, recommending marriage as a way of regularizing the situation and avoiding debauchery.[4]

Christopher Dawson, describing the weakness and disorder of Church life during this period, states that "even in the monasteries the rule of chastity was no longer strictly observed, while the secular clergy lived openly as married men and often handed on their cures to their sons."[5] The danger of the gradual establishment of an hereditary priesthood is remarked by Philip Hughes. Speaking of "the contemporary practice of clerical marriage," he says:

The married bishop and priest had but one thought—how best to transmit his benefice to his own family. The clergy, if such practices spread, would become a hereditary caste, and the property originally given to the churches for the support of charity be the rich endowment of the privileged few.

After mentioning a number of cases of married bishops leaving their sees to their sons, he concludes: "The old law, that

---

[4] Bernard Guillemain, *The Early Middle Ages,* tr. by S. Taylor, New York: Hawthorn Books, Inc., 1960, p. 21.
[5] Christopher Dawson, *The Making of Europe,* New York: Sheed and Ward, 1946, p. 272.

forbade the ordination of the sons of a priest born after their father's ordination, had fallen into oblivion."[6]

The law of celibacy in the West took its definitive, and as it seems to many, final form in the First Council of the Lateran in 1123, which made the marriages of priests, deacons, and subdeacons invalid. That even this strong legislation did not find easy acceptance is evident from the canons of the Fourth Lateran Council a hundred years later, referring to married priests, priests living in sin, and to abuses concerning the sons of priests.[7] Fairly wide disregard of the celibacy law lasted until the Reformation, when large numbers of the clergy, following Luther's example, openly took wives. The Fifth Lateran Council (1512–1517), refers again to clerical concubinage as a common failing, and warns that offenders are not to be excused on the ground that the custom is, after all, so general.[8] Hughes comments that this ineffectiveness of law was a characteristic of the Middle Ages in civil as well as in ecclesiastical life.

In the Western Church today, the candidates for orders, in the course of their seminary training, receive the order of subdiaconate a year or two before they are due to be ordained as priests. Associated with this order of subdiaconate is the obligation of clerical celibacy. In a solemn moment of the ceremony, the Bishop warns the young clerics of the gravity of the step they are undertaking. He says, "Think seriously and repeatedly on the heavy burden which you desire today. But if you receive this order, you cannot hereafter revoke your decision, but you must forever belong to God and observe, with his assistance, chastity." By going forward to receive this order the young cleric undertakes a

[6] Philip Hughes, *A History of the Church,* vol. 2, New York: Sheed and Ward, 1948, p. 201.
[7] Cf. Philip Hughes, *op. cit.,* pp. 376–378.
[8] Cf. Philip Hughes, *A History of the Church,* vol. 3, pp. 480–481.

solemn obligation to live in chastity, and to devote himself completely to God and his people without ever marrying.

If a young subdeacon or deacon changes his mind about becoming a priest during the remaining year or so of his seminary course, or if for some reason he is found unsuited to the life of a priest, the Church authorities normally free him from this solemn obligation of lifelong celibacy, allowing him to return to the life of a layman and marry if he wishes. However, once he has entered into the priesthood, the Church regards his obligation as lasting until death even though he may give up the life of the priesthood in years to come. If he should enter into a civil marriage and have children, the Church has been traditionally adamant in refusing any recognition or blessing to such a union. There have been recent signs of modification of this firm attitude.

The priest's obligation not to marry has, then, become a high and solemn undertaking, if not essentially linked with his ordination, at least so long established as custom, law, and popular image, that to suggest some modification might seem to be almost an attack on the priesthood itself. In the next chapter we shall see some of the reasons commonly put forward in favor of preserving the law of celibacy. This will enable us better to understand the strong emphasis placed on celibacy in the priestly life and the reluctance of those at the official level in the Church even to discuss the possibility of a change.

3:

THE REASONS FOR CELIBACY

WHEN I HAVE, on many occasions, asked Catholic lay people why they think their priests should not marry, they have generally replied, after some reflection, that priests don't marry so that they can devote their whole lives to the work of God and his people. Many have added that it seems much more fitting that this should be so, and have pointed to the difficulty they would foresee in a priest being divided between the care of a growing family and the care of his parishioners.

This reasoning is a reflection of the advice of St. Paul in the seventh chapter of his First Epistle to the Corinthians. Asked by the people of Corinth for advice about marriage, he gives them some practical counsel on mutual rights of husbands and wives, and then goes on to say, "I wish you were all in the same state as myself, but each of us has his own endowment from God, one to live in this way, another in that." He continues with practical advice about married folk and virgins, reflecting somewhat the common belief of his people that the world would soon be at an end with the second coming of Christ on earth. He says,

Brethren, I would say this; the time is drawing to an end. Nothing remains but for those who have wives to remain as though they had none, those who weep must forget their tears and those who rejoice their rejoicing; and those who buy must renounce possession, and those who take advantage of what the world offers must not take full advantage of it; the fashion of this world is soon to pass away. I would have you free from concern. He who is unmarried is concerned with God's claim, asking how he is to please God, whereas the married man is concerned with the world's claim, asking how he is to please his wife, and thus he is at issue with himself.

St. Paul seems here to be giving practical advice to new Christians who were convinced that their Lord was coming soon to usher in the full glory of the messianic kingdom. Detachment from the cares and concerns of this world should mark their way of life. It may, therefore, seem rather artificial to detach the last sentence of the quotation out of its context and to erect it into the guiding principle for the life of priests of a later age. However, in giving this advice, St. Paul may have had in mind the tradition recorded in St. Matthew's Gospel (19. 9–12) of the occasion when the disciples suggested to Jesus that maybe it was better, in view of his condemnation of divorce and adultery, not to marry at all. "That conclusion," Jesus said, "cannot be taken in by everybody, but only by those who have the gift. There are some eunuchs who were so born from the mother's womb, some were made so by men, and some have made themselves so for the kingdom of heaven. Take this in, you whose hearts are large enough for it." He may have had in mind also the occasion told in St. Mark's Gospel (10. 29) when Jesus told the apostles of the fruitful reward given to those who left home and family "for my sake and the sake of the Gospel." St. Paul, however, in the practical directives given in his pastoral epistles, presumes that the leaders of his new Christian communities will normally be married men with families. He says in his First Epistle to Timothy,

The man who is to be a bishop, then, must be one with whom no fault can be found, faithful to one wife, sober, discreet, modest . . . he must be one who is a good head to his own family, and keeps his children in order by winning their full respect; if a man has not learned how to manage his own household, will he know how to govern God's church? (I Tim. 3. 2–5).

He gives Timothy similar advice for the choosing of deacons, and repeats this counsel substantially in his Epistle to Titus.

We see clearly enough that while Paul seemed to expect that his clergy would usually be married men, there was, at the same time, a tradition coming from the words of Jesus that it was possible and good not to marry in order to be totally devoted to the kingdom of God. This led to the double tradition of having both married priests and priests dedicated through celibacy; this double tradition has remained valid, approved, and cherished within the Church even to the present day.

Before going on to treat of the reasons given at present for the compulsory celibacy of the priests of the Western Church, it is well to make a clear distinction between religious priests and those who are called secular or diocesan. The religious priest has a double form of dedication. One of these derives from his membership in a religious order, an institution within the Church whereby Christians, whether priests or lay people, may form into groups, devoting themselves to a higher striving for holiness through the evangelical counsels of poverty, chastity, and obedience. Those members of religious orders who are priests have not only the obligation from Church law of priestly celibacy, but also an obligation from their personal vow of chastity taken within their religious community.

Our concern throughout this book is, therefore, solely with the secular or diocesan priests who take no personal vow, but have their obligation of remaining unmarried solely from the positive law of the Western Church. It is in this sense that we shall speak throughout of priestly celibacy. About two-thirds of the priests of the West are secular priests. A different view of the celibacy of the secular priest, as a dedication implicitly and appropriately expressed in a vow, is offered by Wilhelm Bertrams in a recent study of celibacy; this book deals with many controverted theories of celibacy, particularly from the canonical viewpoint.[1]

Perhaps the best expression of the reasons commonly given for the law of celibacy is provided in the various papal documents of our time. A review of the documents from recent Popes relating to the priesthood provides us with some surprises; the first of these is in a letter of exhortation to the Catholic clergy written in 1908 by St. Pius X (*Haerent Animo*). This exhortation, covering over seven thousand words, deals solely with the holiness of the priesthood and the means priests should take to gain a deeper and more worthy spiritual life. It is strange to find that this long letter contains no direct mention of priestly celibacy. As we shall see, the development of modern thought on this subject is all in the direction of placing celibacy in the central focus of priestly dedication and holiness.

A later and longer document is provided by Pope Pius XI, and is dated 1935 (*Ad Catholici Sacerdotii*). This is a full encyclical on the Catholic priesthood. It deals rather briefly with the matter of celibacy, pointing out that clerics of the Latin Church in higher orders are bound by this grave obligation. The Pope then develops a line of reasoning on a natural basis. He says, "Since God is a spirit, it is only fitting that he who dedicates and consecrates himself to God's service should in some ways divest himself of the body." He later develops this theme from the supernatural viewpoint by stressing that "priests have a duty which in a certain way is higher than that of the most pure spirits who stand before the Lord. Is it not right then, that he lives an all but angelic life?" This line of reasoning has little appeal for most mod-

[1] Wilhelm Bertrams, *The Celibacy of the Priest,* tr. by P. Byrne, Westminster, Md.: Newman Press, 1963, pp. 42–64, 86–88.

ern authors, who are concerned that the dedication of celibacy should be viewed as a consecration of the whole person,
the synthesis of body-soul, rather than one of spirit alone.

Pius XI develops his central argument along the line of
the priest's dedication to the Lord:

> A priest is one who should be totally dedicated to the things of
> the Lord. Is it not right, then, that he be entirely detached from the
> things of the world, and have his conversation in heaven? A priest's
> charge is to be solicitous for the central salvation of souls, continu-
> ing in their regard the work of the redeemer. Is it not, then, fitting
> that he keep himself free from the cares of a family, which would
> absorb the great part of his energies?

He derives this theme from a kind of moral exigency of
the Gospel and the apostolic teaching. He repeats St. Paul's
argument of undividedness, which we have already discussed,
and goes on to give quotations from the Fathers of the
Church, extolling the pure life expected of the priest.

Another long document on the priesthood is the exhortation on the holiness of the priestly life addressed to the
Catholic clergy by Pius XII in 1950 *(Menti Nostrae)*. Once
again celibacy is dealt with rather briefly. The Pope develops
a strong argument for priestly celibacy from the ministerial
work of the priest:

> The priest's ministry is concerned with the affairs of the super-
> natural life; he forwards its growth and makes it to share in the
> mystical body of Jesus Christ. He must, therefore, bid farewell to
> the things of the world in order to care only for the things that
> belong to the Lord. To ensure his emancipation from worldly cares
> and his complete freedom for the service of God, the Church has
> established the law of celibacy, whereby it might be made more and
> more manifest to all that he is God's minister and the father of
> souls. By this law the priest does not lose the office of a father;
> rather, he enhances it immeasurably in that he brings forth children,

not for this earthly and fleeting life, but for the life of heaven which will last forever.

This argument develops the dedication of celibacy a stage further, and relates it much more clearly to the work of a priest, which demands his complete freedom for God's service, and has in itself a kind of supernatural fertility. The Pope adds a further notion of the likeness of the priest to Christ himself: "The more brightly the chastity of the sacred minister shines, the more completely does he become, along with Christ, a pure victim, a holy victim, an unblemished victim." A striking feature of this Pope's treatment of celibacy is the long negative section warning of the dangers to the celibacy of the priest, a theme to which he returns near the end of the letter in dealing with seminarians training for the priesthood.

Our greatest surprise in reading these two official documents on the holiness of the priest is that in them the celibacy of the Western priest is supported by such slight reasoning. In neither of them is celibacy clearly and firmly presented as a form of dedication in love. While both documents deal at length with the holiness required of a priest, and, particularly in the letter of Pius XII, the bond of dedicated love to Christ is emphasized as the center of the priest's life, there seems to be no attempt to link celibacy with this love.

THE CONTRIBUTIONS OF MODERN PSYCHOLOGY

In view of the modern writing to which we shall be referring, a good deal of which was already in publication before these papal statements, it is difficult to realize why celibacy should be so understated. A priest friend, in discussion with me recently, suggested that the probable reason for this was that the type of writing I had in mind has been derived mainly from the growth of understanding of the dynamics of human development provided by modern psychology. This psychology, owing so much to the influence of Freud and his disciples, has been regarded with suspicion in Rome until comparatively recent days. However this may be, it is undeniable that Freud has presented to the world, and particularly to the priest, the basic insight for an understanding of the development of the human person which throws a strong light on the central importance of celibacy in the life of the priest. It is true that a great deal of Freud's earlier theorizing, particularly in the field of philosophy, has not stood up well to modern criticism. It is also true that much of the more reflective writing of his later years is still subject to argument and adaptation. The important fact remains that his insight into the dynamism of personality development and growth has been the basis for a growing revolution in our understanding of human beings and their needs.

When we separate from Freud's writing some of his own native prejudices and the style of his mythology, we are left with certain basic assumptions or postulates which have had a dominating influence on the recent growth of psychology. Among these basic postulates is that of the central importance of sexual development in Freud's wide sense of this term. The whole growth of sexuality in the human being, from early childhood to adulthood, has a strong influence on the dynamism of close interpersonal relationships in adult life. This insight, still being developed by modern psychologists of both Freudian and non-Freudian schools, has given a base for a tremendous development in our understanding of marriage. The renewal of the philosophy, psychology, and theology of marriage has a central significance in the understanding of the relationship between the dedication of the priest to the person of Christ and the freely undertaken commitment of personal celibacy which is the theme of this book.

The growth toward mature sexuality in man and woman, and the varied expressions of love which come from the dynamism of this growth into manhood and womanhood, are of great significance in our understanding of both the development and the life-problems of human beings. In particular, the potential of expressing the highest human values of love in the stable interpersonal relationship of marriage gives us a kind of measure of full human development. Nuptial love, with its demand on the maturity of each partner, with all its possibilities of self-growth through outgoing tenderness for the other, and its high creative potential, has become a symbol of personal integration and achievement, a standard by which other forms of love and interpersonal dedication, other life-ideals, might be valued and measured.

This is not to say that all interpersonal relationships, all forms of love-dedication, are basically sexual in the narrow sense, but rather that they can often be best explained, codified, and evaluated in terms of sexual imagery and symbolism. That this leads to misunderstanding is obvious enough in the charge of pan-sexualism made against much of modern psychological writing. For all the value of this framework of thought and evaluation, the danger of misunderstanding is always present for those not familiar with its style and inner meaning. There is the further danger, when religious values are presented through a sexual imagery, that emotionally disturbed people will be unable, by reason of their inner tension and confusion, to see through the imagery to an acceptance of the values it is meant to illustrate; their confusion may be heightened by a too literal understanding of what to other people appears as beautiful imagery.

In fact, I consider it a far more intelligent criticism of Freudian and neo-Freudian psychology to say that, far from being pan-sexual, it is not sexual enough. Many later psychologists have pointed to Freud's poor understanding of the psychological growth of women, and it might be said of many

of the modern psychologists that they tend to provide a
psychology of human beings rather than of men and women,
of children rather than of boys and girls. Too little attention
seems to be given to the characteristic developments, problems, and values of boyhood and girlhood, of manhood and
womanhood. This may well be a reflection of the low value
put on manliness and womanliness in our Western societies.

In spite of the difficulties in the use of sexual imagery to
illustrate religious values, the writers of the Old Testament
had no hesitation in presenting the relationship between God
and his chosen people in sexual terms. The recurring theme
of the Old Testament is God's covenant with his people . . .
"I will be their God, they shall be my people." The love
and fidelity which should mark this agreement on both sides
is obviously in no way sexual, but it is presented again and
again in the terms of courtship, marriage, and marital infidelity. The positive idealism of nuptial love is beautifully
used for this purpose in the Song of Songs. Jeremias, Ezechiel,
and Osee, on the other hand, refer bluntly to Israel's infidelity to the covenant as adultery and prostitution:

> All the world heard the fame of thy loveliness; I made thee so
> fair, says the Lord God, utterly fair. Fatal beauty, fatal renown,
> which emboldened thee to play the harlot, lavish thy favours on
> every passer-by, and be his . . . thou wouldst build thee a brothel,
> a common stew, in every street; no cross-roads but should carry the
> blazon of thy harlotry. (Ezechiel. c.16 vv. 14, 15, 24. See also Eze-
> chiel, c.24; Jeremias, c.3; Osee, c.2 and c.3.)

This familiar nuptial imagery is used again for the new
covenant in the wedding parables and incidents of the Gospels. St. Paul uses it to emphasize the close union of dedicated love between Christ and his body the Church, and to
draw from the total dedication of this love of Christ for his
bride, a practical lesson for husbands and wives:

You who are husbands must show love for your wives, as Christ showed love to the Church when he gave himself up on its behalf. He would hallow it, purify it by bathing it in the water to which his word gave life; he would summon it into his own presence, the Church in all its beauty, no stain, no wrinkle, no such disfigurement; it was to be holy, it was to be spotless. And that is how husband ought to love wife . . . (Ephesians. c.5 vv. 25–28).

St. John re-echoes this bridal theme to refer to the new covenant, which he expresses in the traditional terms of the Old Testament:

And I, John, saw in my vision that holy city which is the new Jerusalem, being sent down by God from heaven, all clothed in readiness, like a bride who has adorned herself to meet her husband. I heard, too, a voice which cried aloud from the throne, Here is God's tabernacle pitched among men; he will dwell with them, and they will be his own people, and he will be among them, their own God. (Apocalypse, c.21 vv. 2–4).

It is interesting to note that the present Vatican Council, in its Constitution on the Liturgy, also refers to the Church as the bride of Christ.

Here, then, is a continuous picture of the love of God for his people, love in its highest possible form, the love of the Holy Spirit. There is, too, the response of love from the community of men to God. In Christian times, this responsive love has also a high divine quality in spite of the infidelity of men, for the Church is the body of Christ, identified with him, men united in the new head of their race, who is Christ. The Church is thus able to love the Father in the ever-faithful love of his Son, a love energized in men by the Holy Spirit of divine love. This finally-perfect love is, for the Christian, a supernatural dynamism at the center of his being, adding a high quality to every form of natural human love in his life. For him, love appears not only as the highest upward achievement of his natural being, but even more as a personal gift from above, lifting his life to a level of fulfillment and integration of which he would not be capable on his own. This personal gift within him, the Holy Spirit of God, gives a new radiance and quality to the sexual love of marriage and to every other form and shape which love can take.

This gift of love from on high, in its community form in the Church, and in its personal form in the indwelling Spirit, defies description and definition, reaching as it does into the center and origin of reality in the interpersonal life of the Trinity. So we try to reach it with our minds through image, sign, and symbol. In the Bible we find not only the marriage imagery, but also a number of other images of interpersonal love woven round the person of Jesus. We see him as the dedicated and suffering servant of his Father and of his people; we find him telling his apostles to be the servants of one another in love; he calls them his children, his friends, for whom he is preparing a home with his Father; he tells them of the love which he and his Father have for them; he prays to the Father that "the love thou hast bestowed on me may dwell in them"; he lets them know that his death is a free and personal dedication of his love for them.

This indescribable love presents us with a challenge of love in response, a love which should be a total dedication of our being. On our part, too, we think of loving service of God and our fellowmen, of intimate loving friendship, of total consecration of our lives even to the point of death. When Christians marry, the totality of their love-giving to one another is, at the same time, their common response of love to God; their united love is at once a gift of the Holy Spirit within them, and a joint offering of themselves in return, expressed in the act of sexual union and in the whole orientation of their common life.

CELIBACY AS A TOTAL DEDICATION OF LOVE

While the interaction of love of which we have been speaking is the common gift and challenge of every Christian, it is inevitable that the marriage imagery used to describe the covenanted love between God and his community should be applied in a special way to those who forego marriage to dedicate the whole energy of their life to God and the community in consecrated service. For there is in their case, as with married people, the same possibility of the uplifting of the whole love-energy of their being into their personal consecration. As we shall see, this marriage-idealism of love is directly referred to in the ceremony which the Church uses for nuns taking their vows. They are described in the prayers as the brides of Christ, who, while recognizing the high love-value of marriage, have accepted this meaning and transferred it directly in their dedication to God. Ideally, this is a total and eminent fulfillment of their sexual drive and of its values of womanliness, in a total dedication of their person in love. Their love steps up into the higher order of being and value which we have described in the love of God for his people; it is the focusing in one human being of the whole community response of love to Christ—the nun is the representative of the Church-community as the bride of Christ.

While the love of the nun for Christ is a full expression of her womanhood, it is not in any narrow sense a sexual love; it is something of a higher order than a woman being in love with a man. The philosophers tell us that in the order of natural being, the higher forms contain, fulfill, and surpass the potential of being and value in the lower forms; so, for example, the human level of being contains, fulfills, and surpasses the lower levels of animal, plant, and matter. It seems to be the same with love—the higher level of divine-

shared love in a human being is capable, in certain circumstances, of natural maturity and dedication, of fulfilling and
surpassing the values and needs of sexual and other human
love. The operation of this mechanism at the psychological
level, its limitations and characteristic problems and dangers, is a wide subject which belongs to the proper field of
the psychology of religious women, and not to this book.
The sole emphasis here is to show the link between the
nuptial imagery used to portray the love of God for his
people, and the same imagery used to illustrate the community love and service of a dedicated Christian.

When the celibate Christian is a man instead of a woman,
the same synthesis of divine love and total personal consecration is possible. While it is meaningful to speak of this as a
nuptial love, we usually seek a different imagery in order to
prevent confusion. For the role of the celibate priest is essentially masculine, and he tends to see his role as one identified
with that of Christ rather than of the bridal Church. In the
imagery developed round the person of Jesus in the Bible,
he finds the inner meaning of his own personal consecration,
of the totality of the love which leads him freely to give up
marriage for the whole-hearted service of God and his people.

These ideas received an early discussion as far back as
1927 in the work of Dietrich von Hildebrand, translated into
English in 1930 as *In Defense of Purity*. Von Hildebrand, a
philosopher rather than a psychologist, deals with the whole
meaning of sex for man and woman, with the concept of
purity in sexual life as shown in the unmarried, in married
people, and in the Christian virgin. While his theme does
not directly touch on the celibacy of the priest, his understanding of the kind of central dedication of sex involved in
the personal commitment to Christ of dedicated virginity
provides a close analogy with the personal dedication of the
priest in his celibacy. He points out that this nuptial relation-

ship between the consecrated virgin and Christ is basically the same for the monk and the priest. He says that the priest represents this relationship in a somewhat modified form inasmuch as he primarily represents Christ, not the Church, as the bride who conceives by his gift.

The picture of the Church as the bride is one that is strongly based in the tradition of the Christian people and, indeed, of the Jewish people long before the time of Christ. It is this nuptial relationship which the consecrated Christian undertakes through a deeply personal commitment in the religious life and in dedicated celibacy. This relationship is offered as a gift of love to all Christians, whatever their vocation; it receives a high totality and an outward community-form when placed at the service of the Church in the vow of the religious life or the celibacy of the priest. The Second Vatican Council, in its Constitution on the Sacred Liturgy, speaks of the Church as the beloved spouse of Christ, as the beloved bride who calls to her Lord.

Von Hildebrand points out that this bridal relationship is common to all Christians. He says, "Like the church herself, every member of Christ's mystical body is a bride of Jesus. Jesus is the bridegroom of every soul which is a member of his mystical body."[2] It is within this basic theme that von Hildebrand develops and explains St. Paul's text on the undividedness of the Christian virgin. He points to the deep relationship of dedicated love which is the ideal fulfillment of sex in man and woman; the parties live totally for one another and long to be fully united with one another. Reflecting his earlier reasoning that the marriage of Christians is not an upward evolution from the animal kingdom so much as a devolution from the heavenly kingdom, a reaching down of the holy love of the Trinity, he points out that not only

[2] Dietrich von Hildebrand, *In Defense of Purity,* Baltimore: Helicon, p. 140.

in the Song of Songs but also in the wedding themes of the Gospels we have represented to us the call of love from Jesus to the Christian soul.

In successive chapters he deals with the dedication of virginity under the theme of undividedness, of total renunciation of the highest of earthly values, as a distinctive deed of love forsaking all for the love of Jesus. He leads up to his final synthesis, that consecrated virginity is a marriage with Jesus. He says, "Sex is the secret of every human being, and the disclosure of this secret to another creature and the delivery of it to that other in wedlock constitutes a self-surrender and self-donation of a wholly unique kind." He points out that in the sexual union of marriage the donation of self can be made in a way which involves the entire man as a complete unit, constituting a bond of union that is distinctive and permanent. He continues,

The act which places this sexual secret in the hands of Jesus inviolate and forever, denotes a self-surrender to him and a marriage with him which corresponds with the matrimonial surrender to a creature . . . that supreme self-surrender of the entire person . . . is here made to Jesus by the vow never to disclose this secret to anyone, by the radical and final renunciation for his love of all exercise of sex, cutting oneself off from the world to live for him alone. Only those who have grasped the utterly central position occupied by sex, its depth, and the mystery that invests it . . . are in a position to grasp the mysterious factor which makes consecrated virginity wedlock with Christ.[3]

The dedicated celibacy of the priest contains, as we have seen, the same essential reality as this relationship described for women as a marriage with Christ. Marriage is for human beings the full external embodiment of nuptial love, the highest, most intimate and most central relationship between human persons. It is not surprising that what Pius XI called

---

[3] Hildebrand, *op. cit.*, p. 185.

the highest glory of the Christian priesthood should find meaning in the highest form of love known between human beings. This high relationship of the Christian person with Christ is expressed in the liturgy for the profession of nuns:

Without detracting from the honour of wedlock, and thy nuptial blessing resting still on the holy state of matrimony, thou has yet willed that chosen souls of loftier purpose should reject the bodily intercourse of men and women, but attain the secret that it comprehends; who do not copy what marriage does, but devote their entire love to the mystery which it signifies. Blessed virginity has recognized its author and, envying the integrity of the angels, consecrates itself to the bridechamber of him who is at once the bridegroom and the son of perpetual virginity.[4]

It is only when seen as a total dedication of love and service centering in the inner core of the person that the celibacy of the priest takes on its proper meaning. This interpersonal relationship between the priest and Jesus contains the same element of high dedication as the bridal relationship of perfect love and totally dedicated service which exists between Christ and his Church. The divine-human relationship finds a human form not only in the love between husband and wife, but also in the dedication of love which the priest makes to his Lord. It is within the framework of this total consecration of the person that the priest serves his Lord and his people. It is because of the fruitfulness of this total love that he can be, as Pius XII tells us, the father of his people.

It is this view of priestly dedication in celibacy which is expressed in Cardinal Suhard's letter on the priesthood:

Chastity is love and a sign of love . . . there is only one force in the world which is strong enough to overcome love, it is another love, a stronger love. By giving up human love, the priest gives to such souls as are not blinded by prejudice—and even in the long

[4] From the Roman Pontifical.

run to them—evidence of a unique discovery of happiness that is possible and can be found . . . you see, then, my dear brethren, the heights to which sacerdotal chastity is raised. It is not merely a form of asceticism, adopted to make the apostolate more effective, it is the gauge of a future kingdom in which God will be all in all, and the anticipation of a spiritualized humanity. It is the sign of the alliance of love which unites man to God in a mystical marriage.

And, later in his letter,

The priesthood was founded by love, it is love itself, our Lord's last great gift. In the light of love, everything becomes clear in the priest. Others in the world have chosen glory, or money, or pleasure. Others consecrate their life to knowledge, power or conquest. The priest has left all, abandoned all and given all. He renounces every good, he renounces even himself. Yet there is one thing he claims, which no one can take from him, one good he wants for himself with obstinate determination. In this human world he has chosen love; he has desired it for himself more than anything else, he wants it for his brethren, become now his only concern.[5]

The references to celibacy during the Second Vatican Council sessions, and some rather startling newspaper comments, have led not only to a great deal of discussion, but to some thoughtful and scholarly articles. One of these, by the Dominican theologian Edward Schillebeeckx, develops the meaning of priestly celibacy more fully. He points out that the ideal of Christian virginity was somewhat colored in the early Church by the feeling of the approaching end of the world, by a certain pessimistic outlook on marriage, and by a low opinion in the writings of the Fathers of everything pertaining to the body. Schillebeeckx emphasizes the priest's close personal bond with the Lord in apostolic service to the Church. He develops celibacy in a Christological dimension, pointing out that Christ was unmarried for the sake of the

[5] Emmanuel Cardinal Suhard, *The Church Today*, Notre Dame, Ind.: Fides Publishers, 1953, pp. 262–263, 343.

Kingdom; he must belong exclusively to the Father and to his people in order to fulfill his messianic task. He speaks of an ecclesiological dimension, explaining that the celibate priest serves the Church in brotherly love and disinterested self-giving, expressing in a deeper meaning the human potency of love. In the eschatological dimension of meaning, the celibate expresses by the sign of his life that the world is advancing towards the final time when God must be all in all; he is the herald of the Kingdom.

Schillebeeckx makes clear that there is no essential bond between the priesthood and celibacy, but derives a close affinity from the evangelical counsels given by the Lord to the apostles, and an intimate tendency in the priesthood towards celibate dedication. He points out that it must be the free dedication of a person who is psychologically mature, a spontaneous recognition of the true value of celibacy. He concludes that while the Church may allow for certain exceptions in her rule, she will not consider changing it substantially unless, through new circumstances, it becomes clear that a category of married priests is necessary for the salvation of men; always celibacy must remain as a sign in the priest of the expectation of the Lord's coming.[6] This fuller theological development of the meaning of celibacy is solidly based in an understanding of the New Testament, and in a thoughtful discussion of the life and work of the priest in his service of the Church. However, as we shall see, the complete picture must take into account not only the glory of an ideal, but also the realism of the human nature in which the ideal takes form.

The common arguments for priestly celibacy, which on their own seem so unsubstantial, find their true meaning and focus in the light of this totally-dedicated, all-renouncing love between the person of the priest and the person of Jesus.

[6] From *Herder Correspondence,* September–October, 1964, pp. 266–270.

We see now that St. Paul's words to the people of Corinth in view of the near ending of their world have a pointed relevance to the priest who still announces the passing of the world and the coming of the Kingdom; that he, too, might be undivided in the totality of his love-dedication, completely intent on the Lord's claim and on holiness. We see, too, a further meaning in the words of Jesus, that those who have given up marriage for the kingdom of heaven may have done so out of a deeper dedication of love, which prompts the Lord's warning that this dedication is not for everyone; those only should accept this way whose hearts are large enough for it.

The common reasoning for priestly celibacy, that by it the priest presents to men a Christ-like image of self-denial, repentance and sacrifice, finds depth and a positive human value within the setting of a total dedication of love and service. Even those arguments for celibacy which center around the practical utility of the priest being unmarried, that this arrangement provides very well for the confidential character of a priest's work, for the difficult work he may do in mission fields and danger areas, his ability to live in simple fashion among primitive peoples, his independence in making what may be at times an unpopular stand—all these reasons find meaning and purpose when seen as functions of the dedicated service which springs from the total commitment of interpersonal love which the priest makes in his celibacy.

The psychologist attempts to explore this mysterious area of total religious consecration from the viewpoint of the natural development of the priest as a human being. He may see fascinating possibilities of studying the way in which the fully dedicated priest finds the fullness of his manhood and of his sexual development in the renunciation of his sexual function at the physical and inter-human level. He will think of the familiar mechanisms of sublimation, identification, and transference. He may attempt, as is his proper function, to rationalize what to the priest is a deep mystery of divine love, the Holy Spirit of love dwelling in his central being and energizing the whole force of his person into a loving response of dedication.

In making this exploration at the natural level, however, the psychologist has a most important function to perform for us. He will emphasize again that the final fulfillment of the sexual drive in man can only be found in terms of a close and intimate interpersonal love. He will point out that any form of sexual commitment, whether in marriage or the priesthood, that is not a true expression of the love-energy of the sexual urge, will become progressively meaningless and frustrating once its initial surface attraction is worn away. This is the meaning behind the saying that chastity without charity is dead. It is only those with hearts large enough in Christian love who can find personal fulfillment in a dedication expressed in terms of renunciation of such a high and central human value; unless this value is replaced by a larger and deeper energy of love, there will remain only a vacuum, an emptiness at the very center of the human person.

It is only when celibacy is undertaken, then, as a deep, mature, and intensely personal choice that it can be fruitful of love in the person of the priest and in his service of other men. It is this final warning of psychology which may lead us to an understanding of why the ideal picture of the priesthood developed in this chapter seems rather unreal when compared with the ordinary life of the average Catholic priest of today. There is, in any human undertaking of high personal idealism, a tension and dichotomy between the ideal and the capacity of men to sustain it at the everyday level of reality. This tension is seen and experienced very forcibly, often with deep anguish, in the marriage of mature and intelligent people. There are two factors which deepen

this tension and anguish in the case of the celibate priest—
his ideal is in itself higher, more demanding, further distant
from the ordinary capacity of men; and he does not have
the warm and intimate support of another human being
in the common effort of daily love. Humanly speaking, he
carries this burden alone.

This basic aloneness of life he shares with all who remain
single throughout their lives. All unmarried people face the
task of finding fulfillment for their deep needs of close
human warmth and companionship. They must achieve satisfying outlets for their need to be of use to others, to be giving
to others something of their own love and idealism. The
priest, if he is not to become an embittered bachelor, must
find in his pastoral work a satisfying human experience of this
kind. These needs emphasize also the importance of a rectory
being made something more than a clerical hotel or board-
inghouse; it must provide something of the warm, homely
atmosphere which every priest needs for his human development.

It is for all these reasons that we must discuss with intense
honesty the difficulties of carrying out in our present-day
world the high ideal of priestly commitment which the
present law of the Western Church demands.

4:

THE DIFFICULTIES OF CELIBACY

IT IS NOT SURPRISING that the noble aim which the Church has in legislating for a celibate priesthood is not perfectly achieved. We know human nature from our personal experience, and from the writings of the social historians who analyze the movement of human affairs through the centuries. When we think of the idealistic concept of a body of some hundreds of thousands of men totally dedicated to the highest form of divine love and self-sacrificing service of man, we cannot pretend to be astonished that the bulk of these dedicated men should find some difficulty in living out their ideal from day to day.

The practical magnitude of this difficulty is highlighted in words recently attributed to Pope John. He is reported as saying to the philosopher Etienne Gilson:

Would you like to know what distresses me most? I do not mean as a man, but as Pope. The thought of those young priests who bear so bravely the burden of ecclesiastical celibacy causes me constant suffering. For some of them it is a martyrdom, yes, a kind of martyrdom. It often seems to me as if I was hearing a kind of plea —I do not mean right here, but from a great distance—as if voices were demanding that the Church free them from this burden.[1]

[1] Quoted in the *Commonweal*, May 15, 1964.

These difficulties were abundantly testified to in the letter on the priesthood of Pius XII in 1950 *(Menti Nostrae)*. In this letter, more than three times as much space is taken up by the discussion of the difficulties of celibacy as by the positive reasoning already quoted. The Pope says,

> Be very watchful, then, beloved sons, for so many dangers beset your chastity, dangers arising from public immorality, from the allurements of vice which are so smoothly insidious today, and finally from the excessive freedom of intimacy which both sexes indulge in, which at times dares to creep into the exercise of the sacred ministry itself . . . in this matter we consider it opportune to give you a special warning that, in directing the associations and sodalities of women, you should behave as priests. Avoid all familiarity. Whenever your service is needed, give it as sacred ministers. And in guiding these associations restrict your activity within the limits which your priestly ministry demands.

In discussing the training of candidates to the priesthood, the Pope says:

> Not only must clerics be seasonably instructed on the nature and demands of priestly celibacy and chastity, but they must also be forewarned of the dangers which will confront them. They should be encouraged from their tender years to guard against danger by having recourse to the methods of controlling concupiscence which the masters of the spiritual life suggest; for their progress in other virtues will be greater and the fruit of their priestly labors more abundant, in proportion to the firmness and constancy they show in controlling their passions. Should any cleric manifest propensities to sins in this matter which within a reasonable period he has not been able to master, he must be sent away from the seminary before taking sacred orders.

This heavy negative emphasis seems to indicate an awareness on the part of the Pope of the difficulties which the priest of today can experience in the fulfillment of his celi·

bacy dedication. The widespread disregard of the celibacy law among priests of earlier times, particularly in the early Middle Ages, reminds us how slow has been the development of celibacy as a true way of life for priests. Many factors, educational and cultural as well as theological, have been at work. We would certainly be misreading history if we were to think that the priests of the early Middle Ages were largely a crowd of weak, rebellious and unscrupulous men to whom the faith and the priesthood meant little. On the whole, there was little provision for any professional education for them; as we have seen, our modern concepts of law and an orderly society were in their infancy, in Church as well as in civil life.

It still happens even at present that a law of the Church is accepted by the Catholic community as an ideal to be eventually aimed at rather than an immediate imperative of conscience; if one were to make a long list of all the laws, instructions, and regulations which have come from the Roman Congregations during the past fifty years, it would be surprising to find how many have not been adopted into normal diocesan and parish life. We must not be surprised, then, at what went on in the Church of the Middle Ages, which had neither our present developments in theology and canon law nor our ready communications. We must take into account also the little we know of the thought patterns of the time relative to manhood, maturity, and the exercise of sex.

In the time since the Reformation, factors such as the steady development of the Church in Europe before the threat of Protestantism, a greater attention to the education and training of priests, and the development of law in our society, all helped gradually to bring about a comparatively high level of external observance of the celibacy law. It is not surprising that this progress has been more complete in those areas where the Church has been a minority group facing up to old hostilities. In areas where the Church has been numerically dominant, the gradual acceptance of celibacy for priests has been very uneven; once again we see the important influence of cultural, educational, and group-psychological factors. I have met many priests who have worked in the southern parts of Italy, in parts of Central and South America, in the Philippines; they have told me of areas where the celibacy of priests is still regarded as more of an ideal than a law, and of the psychology of both priests and people who accept this without much question, so that the people have a real reverence for their priest and are surprised at the suggestion that he should live alone. I have not been able to find any authoritative studies of this question; the tendency of Catholic historians to triumphalize the history of the Church, and the old blanket of silence that covers all that has to do with sex, seem to have made us dependent on travelers' tales. However, when one knows the traveler personally as a good observer, even his tales can create a general picture.

A discussion of celibacy, both religious and non-religious, from the viewpoint of sociology, is provided in a recent essay by Joseph Folliet, entitled, "Celibacy and Society." Folliet emphasizes the ways in which sociological factors influence the viability of the unmarried state as an acceptable way of life within any society. He discusses the importance of general patterns of culture, of the typical family structure as conditioned by social, economic, and technical factors, of the value systems of the society, and of the degree of social and individual security. He points to the:

absence of celibacy as a state of life in those societies which we call primitive, and especially in nomadic society. Such social systems can offer neither the minimum division of labor nor the minimum individual security which are essential for the maintenance of such a state. To a certain extent one might look upon celibacy as a sort of social luxury, a consequence, fortunate or unfortunate, as the case may be, of civilization.[2]

While this discussion is not directly concerned with priestly celibacy, but rather with the unmarried life in general, it underlines for us the importance of considering the sociological background to the variations in the practice of priestly celibacy in the various periods of Church history and in the types of present-day societies we have mentioned.

Even throughout the rest of the Western Church of today, where celibacy is the flourishing sign of the common dedication of the Catholic priesthood, the number of priests who fail, leave the service of the Church to undertake other work, and, often enough, contract civil marriages, is far more than is popularly imagined. Priests are normally loyal to one another as well as to the Church, and they help in every way to cover up the public disgrace and unfavorable publicity that may arise when one of their number gives up the practice of his priestly vocation. For this reason no reliable statistical studies seem to be available on this problem. However, when I was spending a year of social study in the United States recently, I was several times informed by senior priests and diocesan officials that the proportion of men who had left the practice of the priesthood in their country was probably about 10% of the total number of priests. This would give an estimate of about 5,700 of these priests among the 57,000 active priests in the United States. *Time*, in discussing the matter (August 21, 1964), gave an estimate of four to five thousand. My native country, New Zealand, with a small and widespread population, is a land of strong social controls and consequent firm community pressure on the priest towards outward conformity; it is

[2] J. Folliet, "Celibacy and Society," in *Celibacy: Success or Failure*, A. M. Carre, ed., Cork: Mercier Press, 1960, p. 26.

estimated in this country that the number of priests who had left the ministry would be less than 5% of the priests working in the country.

The sad psychological and spiritual condition of these priests who have failed to live up to the strong demands of their vocation is well described in a moving little book called *Shepherds in the Mist* by E. Boyd Barrett:

> Stray shepherds would not in so many instances become involved in bewildering entanglements, were it not for the fact that, immediately following their flight from duty, the rebound from their ecclesiastical state to their new worldly life is sudden and upsetting. Many are carried off their feet by the gale of new experiences that strike them. In confusion and excitement, they act on impulse. They grasp at anything they think will hold . . . they cannot look on life steadily or see it whole. The old landmarks whereby they guided themselves are gone. Some rashly align themselves with other churches. Some not only rashly, but with foolish improvidence, contract civil marriages. A few follow perilously close in the footsteps of charlatans and thieves. Some are victims of a shallow infatuation.[3]

CELIBACY NEEDS SOUND BASIS

Celibacy can provide a meaningful and deep dedication for the life of a priest only within the framework of a sound theology of sex and marriage. There must be, too, a correspondingly thoughtful understanding of the psychology of personal development and maturation, especially in terms of the fruitful fulfillment of the sexual drive in close interpersonal relationship. It is conversely true that where this understanding of theology and psychology is lacking, the whole institution of celibacy must be on a weak and faulty basis. Historically speaking, celibacy grew in an atmosphere of

[3] E. Boyd Barrett, *Shepherds in the Mist,* London: Burns & Oates, 1950, p. 46.

an undeveloped theology of marriage and almost total ignorance of the psychology of personal growth. Much of the early praise of celibacy for priests seems to us nowadays as unreal, fanciful, and tainted with a kind of false angelism which presumes that the perfection of man consists in imitating the angels, in trying to be purely spiritual by living a life apart from the body, treating his body as a dangerous enemy of his spiritual progress.

This anti-corporeal, anti-material philosophy of man has been one of the mainstreams of thought throughout recorded history. The Church has always reacted against it officially whenever it has attempted a purist reinterpretation of central Christian doctrine on the Incarnation and the sacraments, particularly the sacrament of marriage. However, this stream of thinking has undoubtedly influenced a great deal of the outlook and philosophy of Christian people in a number of subtle ways. We see it appearing and re-appearing throughout Christian history—in the Gnosticism of late apostolic times, in the Manichaeanism of the time of Augustine, in the Albigensian heresy, and as a substratum in much of Puritanism, Jansenism, and of what we in the English-speaking countries call Victorian prudery.

Frederick von Gagern, a German psychologist, comments strongly on this thought tendency. He points out that Manichaeanism and Puritanism are by no means dead, and that he often comes across the view that the spirit is the source of good and the body of evil. He says,

We must not take too lightly the danger of looking upon the spiritual as something that hovers more or less remotely above or around the bodily and tangible. Thus we banish it to the periphery whereas, in reality, it is the flesh that is peripheral and the spirit central. Thus separated from the bodily aspect, the spirit assumes the role of a thing apart and it becomes easy to thrust the blame for evil upon the flesh. It is our mental and spiritual personality that is responsible for our decisions, and thus for good and evil, and not the flesh. It is more correct and honest to speak of the 'weakness of my personality' than to speak of the 'weakness of the flesh' . . . We prefer, in fact, to speak of having a body rather than of being a body. For what we merely possess, is not a true part of ourselves.[4]

He goes on to describe the kind of escapism which enables us to refuse to accept the whole of our body-spirit nature.

One of the main targets of this kind of thought has always been the whole idea of sexual fulfillment, joy, and free intimacy in marriage. There is the characteristic tendency to undervalue marriage as a way of sacramental love and holiness, and to emphasize rather that sexual intimacy and joy is something merely "permitted by God to provide for the spread of the human race." Such thinking inevitably puts a high value on the celibacy of the priest and produces all kinds of tainted arguments in its favor. That this is still a tendency of the present day is recognized by Courtois in a recent comment on priestly celibacy:

Among the reasons given for celibacy, some are more or less tainted by misogyny and Jansenism. These have only too often been emphasized in the training of priests. At the present time when more advanced theological studies have brought out very strongly the holiness of matrimony and the married state, we must try to go deeper into this problem.[5]

This kind of denial of the high value and goodness of human nature can only provide the priest with an unreal and false basis for the whole of his dedication, and cannot but prevent any fruitful commitment of his whole being in love. When even a well-educated, well-intentioned, and otherwise mature young man accepts celibacy within this

[4] Frederick von Gagern, *Difficulties with Sex Education,* Cork: Mercier Press, 1953, pp. 7–9.
[5] Gaston Courtois, *Before His Face,* London: Nelson, 1961, p. 147.

framework of thought and emotional attitude, it is not surprising that it does not fulfill in him its high purpose of total personal commitment.

It seems that many of the priests of today have undertaken celibacy not as a form of total consecration of their being in a relationship of love with Jesus, but rather as a necessary and wise legal condition for entry into the priesthood, which has been their chief aim in life. They accept celibacy not as a final deeply-involving commitment of their being, entered into with the fullest degree of engagement and personal freedom of which they are capable, but because the Church has a law about it—the idealism behind the law, and its practical consequences to them as men in an everyday world, are only dimly felt and poorly understood. This is put very well by Father Leo Trese in a book addressed to priests; he begins a chapter on chastity by saying: "Why did we take the vow of chastity anyway? The obvious and easy answer is that we had to take the vow of chastity if we wanted to become priests and we did want to become priests." Father Trese goes on to develop very positively, out of an understanding of the sexual development of human beings, the totality of the gift of love which the priest should make in his undertaking of celibacy. He goes on:

If we regard our vow merely in a negative light, as a denial of self for the purpose of discipline, or as a penance imposed by the Church to ensure a more efficient clergy—then indeed will our vow be a heavy burden and our temptations a constant crucifixion. Because, of course, there will be temptations. With many of us, the full force of what our renunciation means doesn't strike us until some time after ordination. The sheltered life we led in the seminary, the careful reverence of friends and acquaintances, the eager anticipation with which we looked forward to receiving the tremendous power to consecrate and forgive—all these things brought us to subdiaconate and priesthood by a fairly easy path. Celibacy, we felt, would be a cinch, a small price to pay for our admission to the sanctuary.[6]

Personal dealings with priests for over twenty-five years confirms my impression that Father Trese's picture of the approach to celibacy is substantially accurate. His sentiments have been put to me by priests over and over again, many of them using his very words. This thinking is reflected also from another viewpoint, that of an observant layman, in Michael Novak's book reporting on the second session of the Vatican Council. Discussing the arguments that went on about the possibility of restoring a married diaconate in the Western Church, he comments:

There seemed to be an almost absolute block in the minds of some of the bishops against uniting marriage to holy orders in any form. It seemed to outsiders that the celibacy of these bishops had been so precarious, at least unconsciously, that if they had had the choice, they would never have accepted it. How else explain the claim that if deacons could marry fewer would wish to be priests?[7]

Obviously there have been many Western priests who have chosen celibacy as a full and meaningful commitment to Jesus; but we cannot ignore the feeling of the great number of priests who have undertaken celibacy largely because it is legally joined with the priesthood, and who, as they honestly admit, would not have chosen a celibate life if there were any other way of becoming a priest. Even more serious attention must be given to another group of priests—those of inadequate maturity, and often faulty religious development who have, at the emotional and unconscious level, accepted celibacy precisely because of their own personal inadequacy and sexual immaturity. They have seen,

[6] Leo J. Trese, *A Man Approved*, London: Sheed and Ward, pp. 54–56. Cf. American ed., Notre Dame, Ind.: Fides Publishers.
[7] Michael Novak, *The Open Church*, New York: Macmillan, 1964, p. 123.

often with deep unconscious anxiety, any other form of life as a danger—a danger primarily to their own uneasy psychological and social balance, and, by rationalization, a danger to their eternal salvation. Such priests will often emphasize, with unconscious irony and reversal of values, that they became priests primarily to save their own souls, because it seemed the safest way to heaven, and only then to save the souls of others.

Because of all these limiting factors which we have discussed, and of others still to be mentioned, we should not be surprised at the high level of inner frustration and anxiety evident in the lives of large numbers of Catholic priests. This frustration and anxiety is mostly situational rather than neurotic. Karen Horney, discussing the neurotic personality, speaks of "situation neuroses," which occur "in individuals whose personality is otherwise intact and undistorted, developing as a reaction to an external situation which is filled with conflicts . . . they reveal no neurotic personality, but only a momentary lack of adaptation to a given difficult situation." Horney makes clear that these are not neuroses in the classical sense, and excludes them from consideration as neuroses in her later work.[8]

This kind of group situational conflict is familiar to sociologists and social workers—a group of people, distinguished by race, religion, social class, economic factors, by any of these or some combination of them, are commonly subject to various conflicting pressures from within and without. Some proportion of the group adjust reasonably well to these conflicts by developing a strong inner group life, and barriers against outside pressure. Others, for a variety of reasons, cannot or will not accept such inner supports and tend to internalize these conflicting pressures, with resulting con-

[8] Karen Horney, *The Neurotic Personality of Our Time*, New York: W. W. Norton, 1937, p. 30. Also cf. Karen Horney, *Our Inner Conflicts*, New York: W. W. Norton, 1945, p. 11.

flict symptoms which are so like those of true character neurosis that they are often loosely called neurotic. Those who find little support in their situational conflict from the inner life of their group, and at the same time find frustration and anxiety in their outward relationship to other dominant groups, are the "Marginal men" spoken of by Stonequist and so well-known in practice to social workers.[9]

While there are obvious differences in the case of priests, both as a group and as individuals, we must not be indifferent to the elements of built-in conflict in their situation. As we shall see in the course of this book, these situational conflicts relate not only to their celibacy dedication but also to the areas of training, psychological and social maturation, and role-finding, associated with their celibacy and with their priesthood generally. As the traditional values associated with these areas of priestly life remain comparatively static in comparison with the rapid development of similar and often conflicting values in our mobile Western societies, the conflict pressures from without tend to increase.

As in the case of other social groups subject to conflicting pressures, many priests, through intensifying their inner personal and group life, make satisfactory, and, at times, very fruitful adjustments to meet the challenge of these pressures. Others, without such strong internal support or energy, tend to seek adjustment through various forms of compensation. Still others, as we have seen, react to these stresses in total or partial failure; in many of these cases, their own personality has inner elements of weakness or faulty development which are intensified under these group pressures. There is a wide general tendency in all priests to suffer from a relatively high level of frustration and inner anxiety. Much of this is, of course, at the unconscious level, showing itself externally in any of a large number of outward symptoms

[9] Cf. Everett V. Stonequist, *The Marginal Man,* New York: Russell & Russell, Inc., 1962.

and peculiarities. Much, on the other hand, is openly conscious and will be freely discussed by priests with counselors, doctors, and one another. Many priests, for example, have discussed with me their feelings of the uselessness of their lives, their irrelevance to modern people and society, their feeling of being in some way disappointed, almost cheated, in life. They had come to feel that the theoretical commitment of their forward step when receiving subdiaconate had not really been a deep and solid dedication of their inner person, but only an outward act of conformity and obedience at an immature level, full of the unrealism of a youthful enthusiasm.

The general disintegrating effect on personality that stems from conflicts that are not satisfactorily resolved into energies of new growth and development is well described by Karen Horney:

> Living with unresolved conflicts entails not only a diffusion of energies but also a split in matters of a moral nature—that is, in moral principles and all the feelings, attitudes, and behavior that bear upon one's relations with others and affect one's own development. And as in the case of energies, division leads to waste, so in moral questions it leads to a loss of moral wholeheartedness, or in other words to a loss of moral integrity. Such impairment is brought about by the contradictory positions assumed as well as by the attempts to conceal their contradictory nature.[10]

Many of the priests whom I have come to know, in several countries, seemed to be rather restless and insecure, as if they were vainly searching for some elusive peace of mind and for some way of normal and secure adjustment to the force of their natural drives and energies as men. The opinion of many older priests with whom I have discussed this problem reinforces my own view, that this restlessness, anxiety, and frustration in priests is related to the lack of deep

[10] Karen Horney, *Our Inner Conflicts*, p. 161.

personal involvement and existential freedom in the primary orientation of their life. The modern priest is all too often rather "outer-directed" than "inner-directed" in the key motivation of his life. He tends to accept dominant ideas and directives from outside himself, to be carried, often enough, as a burden and a "cross," rather than to find direction and life-energy from within. His own integrity and maturity, his own personal assimilation to the Gospel message, his own committed response to divine love dwelling in the center of his being, do not seem to be the mainsprings of real life for him.

Whether or not we accept Freud's theory of the sublimation of the sexual drive into other socially-acceptable forms of activity, it remains certain that when the sexual energy does not achieve its normal physical and interpersonal fulfillment it will leave an emptiness in the personal structure which needs to be filled by some form of wholehearted devotion in love; otherwise a man will be unfulfilled, empty, and insecure. If the void left by celibacy in the priest is not filled by a generous and total personal commitment to Christ and his people in loving service, it will inevitably be filled by a devotion to lesser values producing only frustration and restlessness. By way of compensation, the priest's devotion to these lesser values will tend to be compulsive and automatic, dominating his life, and at the same time producing an unresolved tension and anxiety by reason of their contrast with the high personal ideal of the Gospels. Thus the priest whose celibacy is not fully integrated and inner-directed tends to become rather professionalized, callous, and cynical. He will become attached to inferior values such as the gaining of money, of power, of authoritarian domination over others. His life will be marked by a craving for excitement, for "good living," for the novelty of new gadgets and the love of small possessions. The resulting disharmony and the inevitable frustrations he meets can lead him gradually into such negative expressions as petty cruelty, dishonesty, disloyalty, and sexual flirting. All of these substitute satisfactions may, and commonly do, rush in to fill the emptiness left by a celibacy which is not really his own.

Such priests may indeed live a life that seems outwardly blameless enough; Catholic people, and many others, have such a high esteem for the essential functions of a priest that they may hopefully overlook his defects of character and general lack of maturity. Priests such as we have described may be keeping to a perfect external conformity with the Church's law of celibacy for priests, but inwardly they may be empty of any sense of total dedication to the Lord and his people, and filled rather with a compulsive devotion to sensual and spiritual trivialities.

5:

SOME EFFECTS OF THE CELIBACY LAW

IT WOULD GIVE an entirely false view of the priests of the Western Church to consider only the deficiencies evident in their way of life. It is necessary to recognize openly and strongly that there are great numbers of Catholic priests who understand quite deeply and sincerely the view of celibacy which is developed in this book. They make a reasonably satisfactory adjustment to the problems involved in carrying out their day to day living of the high ideals of this total engagement of their being to Jesus in the Holy Spirit of love. While this book is concerned mainly with the many others in the priesthood who fail, in varying degrees, to make this personal consecration and adjustment, it would be wrong to visualize Catholic priests as a group of men who are, on the whole, maladjusted, disappointed, anxious, and frustrated. As to what proportion exists between the various kinds of priests we described, we have, as yet, no reliable estimate.

We have emphasized in the last chapter that some large proportion of priests show a basic lack of adjustment which seems to be related to a lack of inner commitment. It is obviously impossible to state this conviction in statistical terms; it is doubtful whether any kind of social research could provide a satisfactory measure of what is basically a problem of deep, inner personal commitment in response to the supernatural reality of the Father's gift of personal love.

The only large-scale research I have seen on the incidence of mental breakdown among priests was carried out by the Benedictine psychiatrist, Dr. T. V. Moore, some thirty years ago. He found that there were, among the 30,250 priests in the United States in 1935, 135 priests who were patients in mental hospitals. This was a much lower incidence than that for Army or Navy personnel. Dr. Moore states:

> Turning now to the mental disorders of secular and religious priests, we find that *dementia praecox* again heads the list as the most common type of insanity. It is definitely higher than for males of the general population. The next most common type of insanity is alcoholic, 20.74% as compared with 7.3% for males of the general population.

Speaking of the incidence rates of nuns, he suggests that "the excess of *dementia praecox* insanity might be explained by the tendency of pre-psychotic *praecox* personalities to seek admission to the religious life." He also concludes that "evidently an undue proportion of individuals who, to say the least, are paranoid personalities seek admission to the priesthood."[1]

In his later book, Moore uses his previous figures to argue against Freudian theories on the etiology of mental illness, and points out that admission rates for priests in mental hospitals were less than half that for single men in the general population. He concludes: "There is no evidence that a celibate life as such is a causal factor in either psychotic or psychoneurotic conditions."[2]

These figures are, of course, quite inconclusive. Moore's comparison of priests with single men in the general population fails to take into account the very thorough screening,

[1] Thomas V. Moore, "Insanity in Priests and Religious," in the *Ecclesiastical Review*, vol. 2, 1936, pp. 484–498, 605.

[2] Thomas V. Moore, *The Nature and Treatment of Mental Disorders*, London: Heinemann, 1946, p. 87. Cf. American edition, 2nd. ed., New York: Grune & Stratton, 1951.

during a period of several years, of all candidates for the priesthood, in which rejection is made of those of low intelligence and of those whose family history or personal peculiarities suggest obvious instability. Imperfect as this screening may often be, it would undoubtedly be a major factor in any statistical comparison. Interesting as these figures may be in themselves, they contribute little to our present discussion; mention is made of them because they have been widely quoted in discussions about priestly celibacy.

The view we have proposed is that priests in some large proportion, much larger than is commonly thought, do suffer in their inner personal life, and in the quality of their work and service for the Church, from a lack of understanding and adjustment in relation to their celibacy. Added to these are those many priests mentioned previously who fail altogether to live out their lives in celibacy, and retire from the work and life of the Church into some form of lay endeavor and, often, into civil marriage. The number of priests involved in these two groups is clearly more than sufficient to justify honest, open, and expert examination of the celibacy law and its effect on the lives of both priests and lay people. This book aims to be a simple opening statement which would serve as a spur and an introduction for fuller and more expert investigation.

THE PROBLEM OF BIASED INTAKE

One of the most important general effects of the law of celibacy for priests is that it provides the priesthood with a biased intake. Modern work in the field of vocational guidance has shown that every profession tends to attract not only those of a certain type of ability and aptitude, but also those with characteristic personality development. There are noticeable differences between those young men who wish to be medical doctors, and those who wish, for example, to be accountants. As the priesthood is definitely a non-marrying profession, it has an attraction to those young men who do not wish, for purely natural reasons, to enter into marriage. It may be an interesting project for some social scientist to make a well-planned survey of men of age nineteen or twenty, dividing them into two groups—those who plan to marry sometime, and those who have no intention to marry —exploring the common reasons for these decisions and also the common features of personality development and emotional maturity which characterize each group.

There may be many mature and well-integrated young men who do not desire to be married, but we inevitably have among the non-marrying group all those who hesitate to marry because of their lack of personal growth, their high basic anxiety, and their inadequacy in any close interpersonal relationship. Such men often appear to be shy, withdrawn, and remote. Often, through over-compensation, they present an opposite surface appearance of being dashing, socially successful, and sexually irresistible. They very commonly end up as the rather lonely, self-sufficient bachelors of late middle age, considered by their friends to be somewhat old-maidish, undeveloped, and unfulfilled in their manhood. Such bachelors are often reasonably well-adjusted in their work, and in their rather shallow friendships, but they are not sufficiently confident and secure in their relationships with others to be able to face up to the close and intimate union of persons in marriage. They commonly tell us that they value their independence too much to be married. These middle-aged bachelors seem to us very often to be rather cold, unresponsive people, and, quite often, very authoritarian. The central energy of their lives is not love but power; they seem to be eager to own and to dominate people rather than to love them.

The celibate priesthood has a natural attraction for this bachelor type; it seems to present to him the kind of life he could be good at, with an expectation of the high social approval and status which seems to be a deep need of his personality. It is easy enough for anyone who knows priests well to recognize in the above description of the typical middle-aged bachelor a fairly common type of parish priest who lives an outward life of eminent respectability, is fearsomely zealous in collecting money for big projects, runs the lives of curates and parishioners with a code of canon law in his hand, and is the last priest anyone in deep trouble would think of consulting.

The priesthood, as a celibate profession, has a natural attraction not only for the bachelor character, but also for those whose general personality structure is rather homosexual than heterosexual. By this we do not mean the overt homosexual; the difficult seminary training, and ordinary selection procedures, are usually sufficient to keep such men away. We rather mean those who have adjusted reasonably well to their basic homosexuality, of which they might be quite unconscious. Such latent homosexuals seek very often to find some socially acceptable outlet for their sexual drive in various forms of social service; such organizations as boarding schools for boys, scout groups, and boys' clubs recognize this as one of their normal difficulties of staff recruitment. It is a particularly serious one in that a latent homosexual who is willing to help, and is leading a blameless life of high respectability, is often quite inadequate in his inner personal control. He may be unable to cope with his sexual urges in a new and highly tempting set of circumstances. Recruitment for the priesthood poses the same kind of difficulty in that it appears to provide such men with an outlet for their love-energy which has not only no possibility of marriage, but a high degree of built-in self-praise and adulation on this very score; it offers a very desirable level of social acceptability and status.

While those who screen candidates for the priesthood in the seminary can be very able in eliminating the more inadequate bachelors and homosexual types, those whose defects are latent, and unconsciously camouflaged, and who have achieved a fair measure of adjustment with the normal demands of living, can present themselves as model students. They can appear to be serious, zealous, and obedient, highly desirable candidates for the priesthood. It is common experience that, unfortunately, many of them have become priests. They may lead respectable lives, conforming well to the rule of celibacy and the other rules governing the lives of priests. However, because of their inability to grow into manly, mature, well-integrated men, and to form balanced and warm relationships with others, they provide the priesthood with a biased load of rather cold, withdrawn and authoritarian members. They give to the world of men a distorted image of the priest. They tend to give to their people a repressive kind of service based not on the urgency of their love, but on all kinds of awkward rationalizations of duty, authority, and piety.

Those candidates for the priesthood who are within the normal range of mature personality development often tend to fail in achieving their full maturity because of poor presentation of psychology and marital theology offered in the seminary as a basis for their training and growth. Many of them certainly do, on their own initiative, by study and self-examination, rise to a high degree of personal integration and dedication. Some are lucky enough to find experienced and wise counseling within the seminary to aid them. But a great number of them appear, even after years in the priesthood, to be personally unfulfilled, men who have never fully grown up, who have never reached the full maturity of which they are capable. These men are often uneasy in their relationships with women, undeveloped in their own inner integrity. They seem to be somewhat adolescent in their attitudes to sexual matters and, often enough, in their general interests and hobbies.

These deficiencies in the personalities of those coming into the life of the priesthood have been highlighted and emphasized as we have gradually come to a deeper understanding of the dynamism of human development, as presented to us by the various schools of modern psychology. A further highlight comes from the increasing capacity of Catholic lay people in their general education and their professional competence in the fields of psychiatry, psychology, sociology, and social history. Even those fields of study long regarded as the preserve of the clergy, such as theology, Church history, and Church administration, are fast opening up to an emerging laity; this is seen in the increasing number of highly competent books and magazines by laymen and women dealing with these subjects and with critical reviews of many aspects of the life of the Church in the world of today.

This awakening laity is demanding a type of priest who will be much more capable of providing them with the mature religious leadership and counseling which the loving-service of the priesthood implies. It has been very noticeable, over the past twenty years, that the amount of well-informed and respectful criticism of the qualities and habits of the clergy has been growing steadily throughout the Western Church. It seems very difficult to foresee any large improvement in the tensions between clergy and laity without a major overhaul of policy designed to correct the biased intake for the clergy. This bias which we have described provides the priesthood with an overloading of personality types who are basically unsuited for the life and work demanded of the priest in the present day and in the foreseeable future.

A further basic difficulty associated with the law of celibacy for priests is that while marriage, of its very nature, demands a reasonable level of personal maturity and responsibility, the life of celibacy within the strong authoritarian social structure of the Church, appears at first sight to make no such demand. The full ideal of celibacy, which we have examined as the proper norm of priestly dedication, does indeed make a very high demand in terms of personality development and sexual maturity. However, it is possible, and, as we have seen, common for men to enter the priesthood without such an integrated view of their personal dedication and, consequently, to remain at a low level of maturity and development. In fact, the whole emphasis of seminary training as it is now conceived, seems to be rather in the direction of immaturity than of mature responsibility. It seems often as if the Church does not particularly want strong and vigorous characters in its junior clergy, and makes little attempt to develop strong, mature, and responsible men within the walls of the diocesan seminary.

As we shall see in a later chapter which examines more in detail the structure and objectives of training for the priesthood, the general effect of most seminaries at present is to keep the candidates in a state of humble subjection to authority. The emphasis is on ready and instant obedience to a detailed plan of life, and, for the future, similar obedience to those in authority within the Church. That this is no fanciful picture of seminary life is evident from the concern shown by Pius XII in his letter on the priesthood of 1950. He states quite openly that many bishops today are gravely worried over the training given in the seminaries; he stresses that the life of boys in the seminaries should correspond as far as possible with the normal life of other boys, and that

the chief effort should be expended on forming the character of each boy, gradually developing in him the sense of responsibility, a power of judgment, and a spirit of initiative. To assist this development, rectors of seminaries will do well not to be unduly coercive, and, as the youths grow up, gradually to relax the strictness of the surveillance and the various controls. By this means they will induce self-discipline and a sense of personal responsibility. Moreover, they should not only grant a certain freedom of action, they should also accustom the students to think for themselves.

The kind of training for submissiveness and immaturity with which the Pope was concerned would have grave enough consequences if a normal proportion of these students were eventually to enter into marriage. This might help them to develop in themselves a good level of personal responsibility and of mature interpersonal relationships. Allied as it is to the law of celibacy, it provides an inevitable trap, into which those students who have not the inner strength to develop on their own, will view celibacy mainly in terms of obedience and authority. They will fall into the kind of immature dedication which will provide a poor basis for their life of personal commitment and service in later years. It may well be that with the increasing complexity and excitement of modern Western life, this problem of a faulty basis of dedication for the priestly life is intensifying. The proportion of priests may grow who feel the inadequacy of their level of commitment to meet the tension and dichotomy between their poorly integrated ideals and the exciting, rather frustrating pace of life around them. At the best, these priests will continue somewhat doggedly to plod through life rather than experience the full freedom of the sons of God which the emancipation of a total personal commitment in celibacy might have provided for them.

More than a little confirmation of this view is seen in the poor average quality and low professional competence of the various periodicals dealing with the pastoral and ascetical interests of the Catholic clergy. As compared with the material available for those of other professions, these publications, with a few notable exceptions, provide a rather negative and legalistic view of the life of the priest, and demand of their readers only a low level of intellectual effort. It is certainly possible that editors are only being realistic in recognizing the low intellectual attainment and interest in the graduates of the seminaries, as compared with those of graduates of other professional schools. This comparison is sufficiently obvious to be a cause of common concern to priests, bishops, and other Church authorities. It seems clear that one of the major factors in this problem is the same basic lack of commitment and personal responsibility which we are examining in relation to celibacy.

Related to this same problem is that of the rather disappointing work-load carried by the average priest, as compared with that managed by those of the other helping professions. I know that it is a popular image of the Catholic priest that he is hardworking and devoted, that his professional work extends over long hours of unremitting toil. In the judgment of a great number of priests with whom I have talked, this is very generally not so, except in missionary areas in emerging countries. Such missionaries are largely members of religious orders, with whom this book is not directly concerned. My own experience in the priesthood has brought me into close working contact with members of many other professions, physicians, psychiatrists, social workers, psychologists, university lecturers and professors. I am convinced that, on the average, these members of the other professions dealing directly with human beings, their needs and problems, work more devotedly and for longer hours each week than does the average secular priest. In the many clergymen of other churches whom I work with, I cannot but admire the high level of personal dedication to Christ and his work among men which they show, in comparison with the average of the priests whom I have known so well over the past twenty-five years.

This view of the work-load of priests applies particularly in those areas in which priests are relatively plentiful. In many other places, the priest is kept very busy with his routine sacramental duties and with a bare minimum of personal teaching and instruction. However, in the well-developed areas, which have only between 400 to 1000 Catholics to each priest, these essential duties of the priest do not normally take up a very large proportion of his time. He is left to choose his style of pastoral work with a good deal of personal freedom. It seems, in a great number of cases, that he is unable to escape from the traditional role of being chaplain to a relatively closed and inner-oriented Catholic community; very often the duties of this role, arduous enough in the circumstances of a century ago, no longer present themselves with great urgency to the modern priest. Though there are encouraging signs of development, so far he has been unable to define a new and fully-satisfying role in the wider, highly-developed, and more mobile community of today. In relating this problem as an effect of the lack of inner personal commitment in the priest, I am aware that the lack of definition in his modern role itself contributes to his own lack of inner meaning and low level of personal dedication. As in so many human problems, we have the familiar vicious circle of cause and effect.

THE PRIEST'S EFFECTIVENESS AS COUNSELOR

It is worth noting another general effect of celibacy which is coming under increasing attention. This is the relative ineffectiveness which it brings about in the fields of counseling for marriage and education. Counseling of young people in preparation for marriage, helping them to face up to the difficult adjustments which the married life often involves, counseling married people as they meet up with the problems of personality growth and sexual adjustment of later married life, assisting them in dealing constructively with the problems of their children's development—all of this has long been regarded as an integral part of priestly service. However, in our own day, through the revolution of psychology, the whole field of counseling has become a much more expert area, demanding more in terms of the interchange of personalities and the sharing of experience. Counseling has come to be a highly developed form of interpersonal relationship. Moreover, the gradual acceptance of Rogers' basic techniques of non-directive counseling in the fields of marriage guidance, and of dealing with teen-agers, demands of the counselor attitudes of mature responsibility for which priests are, generally speaking, not being trained.

But, however well-trained in psychology, sociology, and social work a priest may occasionally be, however mature in his personal attitudes, he is at a disadvantage when entering this field because of the unusual nature of his own life-experience. This has been a constant feeling of my own over many years of counseling and guidance work, a feeling shared by other priests of similar training and experience. Only recently I was acting as leader of a small seminar of highly qualified professional people discussing plans for further development of work in the areas of marriage guidance, counseling and family education. One of the marriage counselors remarked that her experience was that, in dealing with young people coming for group counseling in preparation for marriage, it was immensely more effective for the counselor to have wife or husband present also, so that young people share not only the ideas of the group leader, but also the living experience of a well-adjusted marriage. "In fact," she said, "this should be compulsory for all such occasions." This met with the general agreement of all present, until someone remembered me and made a polite exception for priests. I assured them that I fully realized that while the priest has many advantages in the field of marriage counseling, this is one of his large disadvantages. The people present then discussed very freely the general lack of confidence felt by Catholic lay people in the teaching and practical guidance given them in the intimate areas of marriage and child-raising by their unmarried priests. The prolonged controversy in many countries over the moral theology of family limitation gives ample testimony of this growing lack of confidence. One of the counselors in my seminar remarked that it would be a wonderful thing if we had even a few priests in the Catholic community who were men with the responsibilities of wives and families; these few could give confidence and realism to the Church's whole role in the field of family guidance.

That this is no fanciful view is shown by the standards for marriage counselors stated by the National Council on Family Relations in the United States. After dealing with professional qualifications, personal qualities are listed as follows:

   A. The candidate shall possess personal and professional integrity in accordance with accepted ethical standards.

   B. The candidate shall have an attitude of interest, warmth and kindness towards people, combined with a high degree of integration and emotional maturity.

   C. The personal experience of marriage and parenthood is a decided asset.

In England, the National Marriage Guidance Council has also stated that marriage and parenthood are assets to marriage counseling, with emphasis that the counselor's experience must be that of a happy and stable marriage.[3]

A psychiatrist's view of this limitation imposed by the priest's life-experience is described by von Gagern:

It is most important that he (the priest) should acquaint himself thoroughly with the problems of marriage and education. His weak spot will be found in his lack of personal experience. At best he is

[3] John E. Cavanagh, *Fundamental Marriage Counselling,* Milwaukee: Bruce Publishing Co., 1957, pp. 14–15.

a theorist whose knowledge is mainly derived from the confessional, and is negatively colored. Furthermore, many theologians find it difficult to attain to a positive position regarding their own sexuality or towards the opposite sex. They have had usually a one-sided education and training, in which little space was provided for the necessary discussion and consideration of these matters.[4]

One of the chief difficulties about celibacy as a universal law for priests is that it may defeat its own purpose. One of these purposes is certainly to show the priesthood and the Church in the light of the renunciation of the high values of this world for the higher values of the kingdom of heaven, as a reminder to all that our time is near when the values of this world must find fulfillment and completion after death. There is always the danger that the priest would appear not only to renounce the high values of marriage, but also to become remote and withdrawn from these values and from the concerns of this life. It is the opinion of many well-informed lay people that most priests are somewhat cut off from the common cares of daily life, remote from their people, uninvolved in the ordinary worries and cares of living. Here is a picture of men who have not really renounced good things for a reminder and symbol of their up-graded fulfillment, so much as despised the things of this world as if they did not matter. Not only do some of these men seem to have little appreciation of the positive values of marriage, these very values which are the substance of their renunciation, but they appear to many of their people as men in an ivory tower, secure, comfortable if not affluent, unreal in their appraisal of the strivings and hopes of married people, unreal and otherworldly in their demands on the conscience of lay people.

I have many times had the experience of lecturing to groups of professional men such as doctors and lawyers, mem-

---

[4] Frederick von Gagern, *Difficulties in Married Life*, Cork: Mercier Press, 1954, p. 11. Cf. also American edition, Glen Rock, N. J.: Paulist Press.

bers of professions in which I have no formal training nor membership. In such lecturing one has always the feeling of being somewhat remote, of being personally uninvolved in the problems of the audience, of speaking from the outside. While this outside view is precisely what is asked for in such a lecture, and can often be of value in a conference of professional men, this feeling of uninvolved remoteness is something that many people consider to characterize the life of most priests in relation to their people.

Because priests do not have the cares, concerns, and responsibilities of married people, because they do not usually work for a living, because they live a life apart, even wearing different clothes, they appear to be withdrawn from the life of normal men. They seem to speak to men as outsiders, giving views that are often valuable as outside opinions, but views that do not come from the experience of normal living.

This is a period in the life of the Church in which it is returning to the sources of its essential life, re-examining the implications of the Gospel message in today's world, re-adapting the social forms which she has developed for her corporate life from time to time. Faced with the problems and difficulties outlined in this chapter, the Church must be concerned with the need for a re-examination of the institution of celibacy as the common law for the great majority of her priests.

6 :

THE DIACONATE AND TRAINING
FOR CELIBACY

A MAJOR OPPORTUNITY for modification of the celibacy law became evident during the second and third sessions of the Second Vatican Council. During the second session the Fathers of the Council approved in principle the restoration of the diaconate as a distinct and permanent rank in the ministry. In the Western Church it had been allowed to become merely one of the formal steps on the way to the priesthood; every priest, during the latter part of his training, receives the various minor orders, then the subdiaconate, the diaconate, finally the priesthood. This has been the only way to receive the order of diaconate, and it has been only in rare circumstances that a man has remained as a deacon and has been allowed to exercise this ministry.

In the Council's third session, in 1964, the Fathers had several votes on the restoration of the diaconate as a permanent function. It was decided that national groups of bishops, with the Pope's approval, could decide for this restoration within their own areas. Married men of mature age could be ordained as deacons, but young men must enter the diaconate only within the framework of the present celibacy law. A proposal to allow young men to be free to marry after ordination to the diaconate was rejected by 1364 votes to 839.

On both occasions when a married diaconate was discussed,

many bishops argued strongly against it; they considered that this might be the thin edge of a wedge towards allowing priests to marry. They also forecast a drop in vocations to the priesthood, in that many young men might prefer to become married deacons; it was clearly in deference to this view that the decision was made to limit the married diaconate to men of mature age who were already married. It is true that the use of married deacons, even older married men, will accustom Catholic people to meeting and dealing with ordained ministers who are family men, and this could have important long-range effects.

It is likely that the restoration of the diaconate will proceed slowly, according to the needs of local areas as seen by their bishops. However, the use of permanent deacons will probably spread from one area to another, as bishops realize the value of having ordained ministers who will assist the priests in many fields of pastoral care, who will be less remote in their way of life, and more closely immersed in the cares of common men. It was urged at the Council that deacons would be a bridge between clergy and laity, that while canonically they would belong to the hierarchy, they would belong psychologically and culturally to the people.[1] While deacons do not have power to offer Mass or hear confessions, they are able to carry out the other sacramental and pastoral work now done by priests; in the early centuries of the Church they were a strong influence in the charitable life of the Christian communities.

In thinking of the married diaconate and its further development, it is necessary to have clear ideas on the Church's present custom in regard to celibacy. When a member of a religious order, who is not a priest, comes to the conclusion that the wisest course would be to try some other vocation, the Church authorities normally grant a dispensation or release from the vow of chastity, so that the religious brother

[1] Michael Novak, *op. cit.*, p. 125.

or sister may return to lay life and be married. A similar course is followed in the case of a young man in training for the priesthood who undertakes the obligation of celibacy at his subdiaconate ordination, and later becomes a deacon. If, for good reasons, he decides that the life of celibacy in the priesthood is not really his vocation, the Church will release him from his celibacy obligation, so that he may return to lay life and be married. It is only when a man is already a priest that the Church regards the undertaking of celibacy as finally permanent in the sense that no dispensations from the obligations are normally granted. Traditionally there is this clear distinction between the celibacy of the priest and that of the deacon. While at present the dispensation granted to deacons is on the understanding that the diaconate, while remaining a valid and permanent order, must not be used as a ministry in the Church, there seems little reason why this must be so, in view of the restoration of the diaconate as a working ministry.

In making the suggestion that the permanent deacons of the future may not only be chosen from among married men, but may, if they are young and single, be allowed to marry as deacons and continue their ministry, we are not making any violent departure from the Church's working traditions. There is no intention of setting aside the decision of the Council against this proposal, but rather of indicating what seems to be a very likely development in the future as experience is gained of the working of the restored diaconate, and the general reform is undertaken of the whole scheme of training for the ministry.

It was reported that over a third of the bishops at the Council voted in favor of young deacons being allowed to marry and continue their ministry. It might be well argued that the majority opinion indicated the wiser course for the present, that it is out of the experience gained from the use of older married men as deacons that later decisions should decide the more controversial issues. However, in view of the whole argument of this book, it seems very likely that permission for younger deacons to marry will be a natural later development as opinion and experience clarify. Celibacy would be, for deacons, a matter of personal choice and vocation. They could undertake celibacy if they felt an adequate response within their being to this form of invitation to fruitful and apostolic love within the Church; or they might freely choose the way of marriage, a less elevated ideal in the abstract, in that it is a less direct form of dedication to the Lord, but one which offers in a different form the same substantial relationship of dedicated love with Jesus to be the centerpoint of personal consecration and service.

The full and final restoration of the diaconate, then, may well come about in three ways. The first, of giving men in training for the priesthood a period of working experience as deacons, is already under experiment and consideration in many places. The Bishop of Arras, in France, recently announced that students for the priesthood in his diocese would not be ordained priests until one year after they had left the seminary. During this year they will work as deacons in the diocese, and will have real pastoral responsibility; at the end of this period they will be ordained priests.[2] This experiment, one of many similar being tried or planned in several places, is an attempt to give further and more realistic training in the pastoral ministry; it will also accustom both priests and people to the work of the diaconate. These experiments will be watched with interest by those who favor an even longer period of pastoral experience before young men are ordained priests and make their final commitment of celibacy. As we shall see, there are strong reasons in favor of a long period of pastoral apprenticeship.

The second form which the restoration of the diaconate may well take in the future is a simple development from

[2] Report in the *Catholic Herald*, London, June 26, 1964.

the first. During such a pastoral year, or longer period of pastoral training as deacons, some young men will no doubt have second thoughts about proceeding on to become priests. This second thinking is one of the aims of such pastoral training. As we have seen, it already happens often enough in the seminary that deacons change their minds, are freed from their obligations, and are allowed to live as laymen. It has been urged that these deacons might be invited to continue their ministry on either a part-time or full-time basis, according to the needs of the Church in their area, at least until such time as they wish to marry.

Even though the Council has decided for the present against deacons being allowed to marry, one could imagine many circumstances in which an exception might be allowed for in cases such as these; we must also take into account that over a third of the bishops at the Council wished deacons to be free to marry, and that this large body of opinion may well grow and develop in the light of further experience. These young deacons who have almost completed the long course of training for the priesthood may have a great deal to offer to the Church; it might seem a great loss if they were unable to do so purely because they wished to be married after receiving the diaconate rather than before. At present the Church makes no real opening for these students who decide in the latter part of their training that they do not wish to be priests, or just that they do not feel capable of undertaking celibacy as a lifelong obligation. Many of them are young men of mature responsibility, well thought of by their seminary teachers. It seems inevitable that eventually the way will be made clear for them to serve the Church as deacons.

The third way of the restoration of the diaconate is that already decided on by the Council and left to the initiative and judgment of local groups of bishops. This decision is the fruit of many years of discussion. Married men of maturity and ability are to be given sufficient training and formation to be ordained as deacons to assist the priests in their ministry. This ministry of the deacons may be on a full-time or part-time basis. The main support for this decision came from bishops in missionary areas, and from those in other regions, such as South America, where priests are few and overworked. Already many missionary bishops have been making extensive use of catechists who have been carrying out much of the work traditionally associated with the diaconate. They are responsible for a Christian community, organize its program of catechetics, its wider apostolate, and its works of charity; they are able to conduct a simple form of worship, to instruct the people, and to baptize, when a priest is not available. Some bishops have been urging for many years that these catechists should be given status and ministerial power by being ordained as deacons. Catechists of this kind are often married men; in many cases they and their families are fully supported by the bishop so that they are free for the full-time service of their people.

Even in areas where the Church is well established, many have emphasized the advantage, in any place where there is some shortage of priests, of having ordained ministers who are married men living among the people. The way for experiment in this field also is opened up by the Council's decision to allow for the ordination of married men as deacons. These married deacons would be able to center Christian life and service around their homes and small chapels; they might provide a way towards that feeling of closeness to the people which is so evident in many of the small religious bodies which in the large Western cities have shown so much vitality and spread of numbers.

The phenomenon of what some sociologists call store-front religion gives evidence of the great need many people feel for a religious community life which is close to them, not only in locality, but also culturally, in being very much part of their everyday living. Daniel O'Hanlon, commenting on the Pentecostals, which he describes as "probably the fastest-growing religion in the world," makes the point that their spread is a natural response to certain basic human needs. They have a special appeal to people experiencing acute social maladjustment, suffering a loneliness for which the large middle-class church offers no remedy. O'Hanlon suggests that "the first reason for the growth of the Pentecostal churches is that when a forgotten human being comes to one of them, he feels himself loved and understood. One Puerto Rican Pentecostal compared the Catholic Church in this country to a supermarket—cold and formal." He goes on to suggest the need for small community churches, each the responsibility of one priest, each small enough for the formation of a true Christian community.[3]

Whether the married deacons of the future devote their full time to the ministry, as do many catechists in mission areas, or whether they support themselves and their families by working in the usual way, their closeness to the people and their very ordinariness would certainly help to break down the barrier of unreality that seems to exist between most priests and their lay people.

It is often urged that the people of the Church could not afford to undertake the heavy financial burden that would be involved in having married deacons working full time with the priests of a parish, and depending totally on the parish for their salary, a salary which would need to be amply sufficient for the support of a family. This difficulty is a real one, but is usually exaggerated. Other churches with a married clergy do seem to manage quite well, and, in many cases, to pay quite reasonable salaries. Many larger Catholic parishes, too, already have several full-time workers on normal salaries, such as lay teachers, parish secretaries, and social

[3] Daniel J. O'Hanlon, S.J., "The Pentecostals and Pope John's New Pentecost," in *America*, May 4, 1963.

workers; while there is, in some places, a tendency to pay these workers very low salaries, in other places there is a regulation that they must be paid rates of salary normal for their ability and experience. A deacon who is married with a family might well contribute more to the life of a parish than do some of the present full-time workers.

However, in many cases a married deacon would need to support his family with little or no financial assistance from parish or diocese. Some people see a difficulty in having ministers of the Church working in some lay field of endeavor during the day, devoting themselves only part-time to a ministry in a parish. This difficulty seems rather unreal. Having ministers who work in the direct ministry in a part-time capacity is so common in the Church that it passes unnoticed. It is quite usual, and fully-approved, for priests to undertake some field of professional work which is associated, often in a rather vague and indirect way, with the general aims and interests of the Church. Large numbers of priests work full-time as social workers, psychologists, psychiatrists, educators, scientists, university lecturers and research workers. Many of these priests earn normal salaries for their work, and it is only in their spare time, usually during weekends, that they contribute directly to the ordinary work of the Church in a parish. There is no reason why a married deacon could not undertake some such work as would contribute in such a general way to the life of the Church, devoting some time during evenings and weekends, as many married laymen do now, to the direct work of the Church.

This work might include visiting the sick and elderly, instructing children and converts, preparing young people for marriage, helping with marriage counseling, preaching on Sundays, and any of a hundred other activities that would make up a valued ministry of the Lord in a parish or city. While a deacon's working life, as we have seen, might well contribute something, through learning or charity, to the general aims of the Church, this is not a necessary condition; if a married deacon were to support his family by working as a carpenter or a fisherman, no Christian would find this strange or contrary to tradition.

We have, then, seen three practical possibilities for the working out of the restoration of the diaconate as a permanent functioning ministry, as decided by the bishops at the Second Vatican Council. None of these suggestions goes against the Church's ancient customs and traditions. To carry out, with due planning and preparation, such programs in the Western Church would cause little difficulty or surprise. It is within the framework of such a restoration that the following proposals are made for modifications in the law of celibacy for the Western clergy.

REFORMS FOR MAJOR SEMINARIES

Modifications in the celibacy law must be seen not only in relation to the restored diaconate, but also with regard to the reformation of the whole plan of training for the secular or diocesan priest. These modifications and reforms should not aim at abolishing celibacy, but at reviving it and renewing it as a form of consecration in dedicated love to Jesus and his people. It should be undertaken by mature and responsible men whose existential freedom and deep commitment is assured and strengthened by their training, learning, and practical experience of the Christian ministry. To make this kind of deep dedication of life possible and common, it will be necessary to provide worthwhile alternative forms of dedicated ministry in the Church, as, for example, the married diaconate.

It must be emphasized, and well understood, that these alternatives are not second-class forms of personal dedication. Philosophers and theologians may well decide that the celibacy form of personal consecration is the highest in the objective order of Christian values. However, in the existential, personal order, the highest kind of dedication any man can make is the one which corresponds to the way that God has made him and is calling him to love, holiness, and service. The man who develops his natural and supernatural capacity to the full in response to the love of the Holy Spirit, and makes freely the kind of commitment that suits his character, personality, and abilities, will be likely to serve Lord and Church with love, devotion and joy. For him, whether he be married or celibate, this is the highest form of dedication to Jesus and his people.

Training for the secular priesthood is carried out, at present, almost wholly in diocesan and inter-diocesan seminaries, and usually consists of six or seven years of specialized education and formation, leading directly through the various orders to the priesthood. Already there has been a great deal of discussion about the eventual reform of seminary training. Because it relates so closely to the kind of celibacy-dedication of which the student will be capable, it will be discussed in detail in our next chapter.

In general outline, the whole system of seminary training would need to be recast if the leading ideas so far discussed were to be put into practice. Chief among these ideas are the practical restoration of the diaconate; the formation of the students towards manly responsibility and maturity; practical provision for a free decision, based on experience of life in the Church's working ministry, concerning the kind of personal dedication which will be most fruitful in terms of loving service.

An immediate effect should be that the intake into the seminary system would be much broader, in terms of the personality range of the entrants. The intake bias of which we have spoken would be gradually eliminated, as young men would realize that the seminary is deeply concerned with their all-around human development as mature, responsible men, to whom will be eventually left the free decision as to what kind of service they are best able to offer to the Church. Young men would understand that, in entering a seminary, they are not making any initial decision about celibacy but are to undergo a formative period of learning, training, and pastoral experience which will fit them for one of the Church's ministries, whether celibate or not; if they consider that they are not suited for any work in these ministries, the training they will have received should fit them for work in one of the other helping professions.

The desirability or otherwise of what are called minor seminaries, at the high school level, does not concern us here; all that we have to say concerns major seminaries only. The structuring of their courses in Western countries already depends very much on the varying relationships of high school, college, and university education in the different countries. It is generally agreed by those who discuss the reform of major seminaries that the first period of training, covering three or four years, should lead the student to the level of a primary university degree, such as the Bachelor of Arts. This should be followed by a period of practical pastoral work, under the working supervision of priests or deacons of mature experience, for one or two years.

This ministerial work should be at a level somewhat similar to that of the present catechists in missionary areas, and may well eventually be an official ministry if the proposal is followed of replacing the present redundant minor orders by a new order of catechist. It has been suggested that this new order could also be received, after suitable training, by religious brothers and sisters engaged in teaching religion, and by lay men and women who undertake training in order to devote some substantial part of their time to catechetical work. This initial period of practical work in the apostolate would provide the candidate for the ministry with the working experience to make use of his studies to this point with a view to development of his personal attitudes.

This experience and development of working attitudes would provide the necessary basis for the next seminary period, covering the ground of the present theological course, which would follow his practical assignment. Lectures, seminars, discussions, and spiritual formation would not be left floating, as at present, in a vacuum of experience, but would be built on the firm base of what had been learned and assimilated in a year or two of practical work with people in the community of the Church. This second period of seminary training, lasting perhaps three years, would lead to ordination as deacons, without any undertaking of celibacy at this time.

The new deacons would be assigned to parishes for pastoral work in their ministry of the diaconate; they would live with priests who would supervise their work and assist them with their continuing studies. This working period in the diaconate should last about five years; during this time the deacons should take part in regular lecture courses, discussions and seminars covering theology, psychology, and sociology at a more advanced level, and sharpening their understanding of pastoral techniques and experience.

During this time, if the further development we have referred to comes about, the deacon would be free to marry if he wishes; if he did marry, he would then, at the end of his training, enter the married diaconate of the Church on a full-time or part-time basis as already described. Those deacons who wished to become priests would do so on the understanding that they must be prepared, in ordination to the priesthood, to undertake celibacy as a full and permanent consecration of their lives. The period of final study for the priesthood would consist of one year's work in a seminary. This would bring the candidate to the priesthood to about thirty years of age before he would make his dedication of celibacy in priestly ordination; by this time he should have reached that stage of psychological and spiritual maturity which would allow celibacy to be the kind of deeply free and meaningful personal commitment in consecrated love which we advocate.

Some such arrangement of training for the ministry as we suggest would not only preserve the celibacy of the priesthood, but would give it the prospect of renewal and revival within a new framework of dedication. However, in spite of the best-planned schemes of training and of pastoral supervision, the inevitable personal mistakes always creep into human affairs; if, at any stage in his life, a priest were to conclude that his attraction towards marriage were such that he was unable to continue his celibacy-dedication with devotion and peace of mind, he should be allowed, as are religious brothers at present, to apply for release from his obligation of lifelong celibacy. Once the proper circumstances of the case are established and the continuing sincerity of the applying priest is assured, this dispensation should be readily given; these priests should then be allowed to continue their ministry as married priests. This would mean that the great majority of the priests of the West would be expressing in their lives the total renunciation of free and dedicated celibacy. There would also be a certain proportion of married priests, made up of these referred to above and, as at present, those married men coming into the Church from the ministries of other Christian churches. There is no reason why married priests would not be as acceptable and useful in the life of the Church as the deacons and the celibate priests.

The Western Church's present experiment with married priests is, so far, a very limited one. A number of married ministers from other churches who have become Catholics, have been later ordained as priests. That this is primarily an

ecumenical gesture does not obscure the fact that it is also
an important experiment which will be studied with great
interest. While there has been, understandably, little publicity given to the working out of the practical problems
involved, the continuance of the experiment under three
different Popes indicates that no insuperable difficulties have
been found. The life and work of one of these married priests
is the subject of a recent illustrated report which concludes:
"The congregation was informed prior to his arrival of their
new curate and his family (of seven children), and they
have been accepted with no apparent reservations."[4]

Quite often, in discussions about the possibility of a married clergy in the Western Church, the experience of the
clergy of the Eastern rites, both Catholic and Orthodox, is
brought forward in arguments both for and against. While
there may be something to be learned from a calm consideration of the long experience of these Churches, this will
certainly not be gained by way of facile surface conclusions
one way or another. The cultural differences involved are
such as to make such ready conclusions meaningless. A much
nearer experience within our own cultural framework, with
similar educational, economic, and social factors at work, is
provided in the married clergy of the large Protestant
churches in our own countries. Even in this comparison,
there are major differences to be taken into account in considering the effectiveness of married ministers within the
Catholic Church.

Those whose lifetime experience of priests has taught them
to regard the celibacy dedication as a mark distinguishing
their own priests from ministers of other churches, find it
difficult to imagine a priest being married and having children. This habit of mind is true of priests and bishops as
well as of lay people. The one recently reported case in the
English-speaking countries of a convert minister being or-

[4] *Jubilee,* May, 1964.

dained as a married priest caused much discussion and heart-searching. It was strange, but somewhat understandable, that it was eventually decided that he would exercise his ministry as a priest in Germany rather than in the United States. This cultural factor makes very difficult any calm and rational discussion of a married ministry within the Church. The suggestions for practical experiment made in this book are presented with full recognition of this difficulty.

In these proposals suggested for further discussion, the Church would have a more varied ministry of orders, as it had in earlier times. There would be ordained catechists, some of whom would be lay people in our present sense, some religious brothers and sisters, some students for the ministry. There would be deacons, married and unmarried, some permanently in the diaconate and others still preparing for the priesthood. Finally, there would be the priests, all at least thirty years old, the great bulk of them dedicated in celibacy, and some few of them married.

While some of these reforms may seem strange at first reading, and very far-reaching, it is only within such a thorough structural renewal that the celibacy of the priest can be given its full meaning and usefulness. That is why, when priests begin to discuss their celibacy seriously, there is always such a wide-ranging discussion. Piecemeal projects of improvement in regard to the life-dedication of priests would be as unsatisfactory as was the similar approach to liturgical reform within the Church; it was not until the Council decided on a thorough renewal of the whole liturgy that such reform began to have true meaning and objective.

The scheme proposed would have the important effect of providing far greater flexibility in planning for the ministerial work of the Church in any country, allowing bishops and seminary authorities to make the best use, for the service of God's people, of the willing dedication of all those who offer themselves for the ministry. In counseling and training those who offer, they would have available different forms of work and dedication to allow for the wide variety of human capacity and endeavor. No violent break is made in the Church's custom and tradition; celibacy is kept as the high form of personal consecration for the priesthood. This revitalized celibacy would present, far more than at present, a mirror-image of the Church as the bride of the Lord, responding to his call of love. Such celibate priests, freely choosing this high dedication at a mature age, would be conscious in their lives of the high values of love, fellowship, and service which they have so deliberately made their own, and which they express in the community as a Christ-sign of the Kingdom which extends beyond the frontiers and values of this world of time.

The effect of such a reform on the numbers of those wishing to be priests cannot be estimated. It was urged by some bishops at the Council that if deacons were allowed to marry, few men would wish to be priests. This is, perhaps, a natural reaction of those whose concept of the present celibacy law is rather negative and legalistic. I see no reason to doubt that if fully-dedicated celibacy is presented to mature men, trained in zeal and personal responsibility, as a true relationship of love in the Holy Spirit, there will not be far more than sufficient men to serve the Church in this way. It is undeniable that great numbers of young men are deterred from the priesthood by the candid realism of their view of the present life of priests as we have examined it in a previous chapter. It is not only priests who are conscious of the inadequacies, defects and frustrations in the priestly life as it is today; what we are beginning to see of ourselves, intelligent young laymen have been sensing for a long time and have been voting clearly by staying away, and going away, from seminaries.

In any case, our attention in discussing the renewal of priestly life should not be centered on the question of numbers, as if the quality of priests, their training, and the intensity of their dedication were secondary matters. We should aim rather at a very thorough renewal in all areas of priestly life and training, a renewal based solidly on the best knowledge and experience available to us. My own feeling is that the number of young men wishing to be priests will increase as this renewal progresses; young men of the type desired for the priesthood are not deterred from their chosen vocation by the difficulties their choice involves, only by difficulties which do not make sense to them.

Even if the fears of some of the bishops at the Council were realized, and the number of priests available became fewer, this might be no tragedy for the Church if the fewer priests were better trained, more mature, more intensely dedicated. The ministerial work of the Christian community is varied, and only a few of its functions can be carried out only by priests. Already many experiments are under way, in a number of countries, in the use of deacons, seminarians in training, religious brothers and sisters, and both professional and voluntary lay people, to carry out work previously done by priests. It is the opinion of many priests that their role in the Church has become far too diffused, and that they would like to devote more of their time to the specific work of their priesthood, leaving much of their present work in the fields of education, fund raising, public relations, and parish administration to others. Many of these priests point to their experience that this diffusion of their priestly role is one of the major factors in building up the frustrations and discontents of priestly life which we have discussed.

7:

THE REFORM OF SEMINARIES

WE HAVE SEEN in previous chapters that the total dedication in love which gives meaning and form to the priest's celibacy is psychologically possible only for those with an adequate degree of sexual maturity and a full understanding of the holiness of sexual fulfillment in the marriage relationship. Unless this understanding and attitude is present in any man, it is impossible for him to undertake such a close and permanent interpersonal relationship with Christ; for this dedication is meant to be a higher form of love, and a living image of the bridal union between Christ and his Church.

That is why Jesus, in speaking of such a dedication to the Apostles in Chapter 19 of St. Matthew, tells us that such a dedication is for love of the Kingdom of heaven and must be accepted only by those whose hearts are large enough for it. If, as we urge, this kind of dedication in celibacy should be the common mark of the priests of the West, it is towards the possibility of such a personal commitment that the seminary should be training its students. By this standard of judgment we must openly admit that most of the seminaries of today are gravely inadequate.

This inadequacy reaches into many other fields, as is inevitable. A training institution which fails to meet the demand of what is the central personal commitment of the priest is certainly failing to meet the other demands of his training as well. In emphasizing the inadequacy of present seminary formation, there is no intention of making any kind of personal attack on those priests who are immediately responsible for the organizing and running of seminaries. They are carrying out a traditional task in a way which reveals often a great deal of personal devotion and learned scholarship. Many of these seminary priests are well aware of the need of reform, which, in the case of some seminaries, is already well under way. While the reform and rethinking I am suggesting is from the viewpoint of the renewal of priestly celibacy, this viewpoint is so centrally important that the suggestions for change will cover most of seminary structure and aims.

That all is not well with the average seminary of the present day is evident by the number and weightiness of the instructions from the Holy See on this subject over the past twenty-five years, and especially by the serious criticism implied in the letter of Pius XII on the priestly life, written in 1950, from which extended quotations have already been given.

We have seen earlier that for the kind of growth necessary to promote meaningful dedication in terms of sex, the young priest, or in the present practice, the subdeacon, should have a good knowledge of developmental psychology and of marital theology. It seems unfortunately true that in both these fields modern seminaries on the whole show serious inadequacies. They have generally failed to promote any notable growth of thinking from the rather ineffective gropings towards human psychology and marital theology of the late Middle Ages. It is because these inadequacies in the theoretical fields are central to the practical difficulties we have seen in the whole way of life of Western priests, and in the quality of their dedication, that it is necessary to devote some critical attention to these studies in the seminary curriculum.

The majority of modern seminaries still seem to pay little attention to general psychology, particularly in relation to child and adolescent development, the maturation process, and emotional stability. Psychology is listed as a subject in scholastic philosophy, which is the major interest at present in the early part of seminary education. However, this is psychology from the viewpoint of the Scholastics of the late Middle Ages, based on a static view of the human being; it is concerned not with the dynamism and energies of his psychic growth, but with some of the philosophical debates of an earlier time, most of which have little meaning for modern man, even for the modern priest. There is emphasis on the philosophical notions of life in its varied forms, of the senses and appetites of man and their relation to his intellect, of the various "powers of the soul," and a rather academic treatment of free will as a philosophic concept in contrast to various outdated theories of determinism. Most priests, in summing up their seminary studies, will point to the psychology course as one of the most disappointing, and one that had little to offer for their own self-knowledge and their understanding of the ways and problems of others.

The fascinating and explosive development of modern psychology has so far made only a faint impression on the course of education provided in the majority of seminaries. We have referred before to the general suspicion with which the growth of dynamic psychology has been received by many within the Church. This has been largely owing to a lack of understanding on the part of many Catholic scholars of the teaching, terminology, and mythology of Freud. The serious attempt to evaluate his teachings from a Catholic viewpoint and to sift out of his writings and those of his disciples the central ideas of relevance to the life of a Christian, has been comparatively recent. But one should be able to expect that the solid work of such writers as Nuttin, von Gagern, Stern,

Oraison and O'Doherty would have made more impact on psychology courses in seminaries. This is not to mention the important work of the other schools and variations of modern psychology, all of which have much to offer to our understanding of ourselves and of modern man. It is amazing to think that so many young men can be trained for the priesthood in our modern day without adequate courses dealing with child development, the energies and dynamisms of psychic growth, the familiar mechanisms of social psychology, and the tried techniques of personal and group counseling.

Because of this fairly general neglect to study man in his individual and social development, the study of the sex drive and of the central importance of sexuality in growth towards mature manhood receives in many seminaries not only little attention, but often real scorn, as if it were a subject dangerous to the spiritual life and vocation of the student. The impression seems often to be given that even the positive values of sex in human development is part of a modern heresy oddly called "pansexualism." Instead, most seminary texts and lectures give a static, negative treatment of sex, interpreting it in medieval language as a matter of the sensual gratification of the passions coming from a force called concupiscence. All of this, on account of the wounding of human nature by orginal sin, represents a constant danger and temptation for all except married people, who are permitted the exercise of sex within modest limits for the purpose of procreation of the race and the alleviation of their concupiscence. Sex is considered in some detail in relation to its sinful aberrations and perversities, and as an influence which can lessen the operation of free will in relation to various temptations. But its positive dynamism in man towards sentiments and acts of love, thoughtfulness, tenderness, devotion and wholehearted interpersonal dedication, is almost entirely overlooked. In fact, the thought that sex can

be a dynamic functioning of human love, closely related to
the love-energy of the Holy Spirit in the center of our being,
would be regarded as dangerous thinking in many seminaries
where I have visited and lectured.

With this faulty approach to the study of man in the psychology of his development, it is not surprising that on the
practical side the average seminary tends towards a withdrawal from the reality of modern living, and an overemphasis on obedient submissiveness. It seems very often
that the manly and masculine qualities of human development are not highly regarded. We must add to this the fact
already emphasized, that because the entrant to the seminary
is already tentatively committing himself to lifelong celibacy, the seminary is receiving a biased intake. It receives
not the average range of developing young men but an overloading of those whose natural interests are away from normal
fulfillment in marriage. This makes more serious the failure
to develop within the seminary a good theoretical and practical program of human development, with research and
practical projects in individual and social psychology. The
seminary often provides a training program which seems to
aim not only at an unmanly, unmasculine personal development, but also at an immature, submissive attitude of mind.
The emphasis is on accepting with little inquiry the opinions of authoritative textbooks, both those of the present and
those of the distant past. Criticisms of the modern society
in which the young priest is to work may be culled from
Scholastic authors writing in Europe in the thirteenth century, or from papal encyclicals of eighty years ago. Modern
writings on the Church, on the ways of our society, and even
modern papal encyclicals find their way with difficulty into
the program of most seminaries.

The average seminary tends to produce a well-informed
and closed mind. The mind of open inquiry, of the dedi-

cated search for truth, so valued in modern university training, is regarded as a dangerous defect in most seminaries. Many priests who have a natural gift of a highly critical, inquiring mind, have told me of the trouble they encountered in passing through the seminary because of the searching questions they asked, because they were not prepared to accept blindly authoritative opinions, not on matters of faith, but in areas of sociology, history, psychology, social criticism, and philosophy.

Training in areas of responsibility and decision-making is usually based on a similarly outdated approach. The seminary tends to place great value on repeated acts of conformity to daily rule, and on the hope that repeated acts of outward virtue, holiness, prayer, regularity and punctuality will develop habits in these directions which will carry the priest through all the normal difficulties of life. That these voluntaristic theories and attitudes have been so widely questioned in the fields of experimental and educational psychology seems to matter little to those authors and authorities who continue to advocate this kind of "will-training." The whole effect of the training given is not toward personal responsibility and the growing ability to make free and well-judged decisions, but rather towards a child-like submissiveness and blind obedience.

The motivation of the students towards learning, towards holiness, towards the priestly life itself, tends to be neglected. Their participation in the learning and training process, and their level of personal involvement, seem to receive little consideration. They are regarded as being well-taught when they are lectured to by someone who has received a degree in the subject, maybe a generation ago, and who reads and comments from an approved text. Seminars, group discussions, research projects, generally have little place. The whole psychological framework of the average seminary is, then,

gravely deficient. This has a serious effect on the progress
of the student towards the subdiaconate, normally reached
about the age 21 to 24 years, when he is expected to make
his deeply personal and totally free decision in committing
himself to lifelong celibacy. It seems clear that very many
seminary students of this age cannot be sufficiently mature
and responsible to make their pledge of dedicated love meaningful for their later years of slowly achieved maturity.

Because of this faulty base in psychology, in many cases
almost a nonexistent base, the theology of marriage receives,
in many seminaries, a poor and negative presentation. Only
recently, after giving a lecture to young priests on marriage
counseling, I was curious to find why their thinking on this
subject was so undeveloped. I turned to the textbook which
they had been using for the study of the theology of marriage, and was horrified to find the outdated approach toward
the sacrament, unchanged since my own time in the seminary
twenty-five years before. It was far removed from all modern
development of thought on the theology of the sacraments,
and ignored the growth of the past fifty years in the theology
of marriage; it showed no recognition of the deeper understanding of the scriptural images of love, betrothal and the
nuptial relationship. It concentrated rather on theses reflecting the controversies of former times, proving that marriage
is a sacrament, that it is indissoluble, that the Church has
power to dissolve certain marriages, that the essence of the
sacrament is the contract between the parties, and so on. One
would think that marriage had nothing to do with sex, love,
or human growth, merely that human beings contracted this
legally-conceived relationship which would, by divine arrangement, bring them the grace to overcome all the difficulties, dangers and temptations which went with the rather
free use of sex permitted within marriage. That sex could
be the central energy of human growth towards interpersonal

love, that it was, in fact, a function of the whole person, that marriage, to be sacramentally fruitful, demanded a growing capacity to give and receive in the intimacy of love, a love which is an image of the bridal relationship between Christ and the Church—this thinking seemed to be entirely neglected.

It is not surprising that, with such a narrow view of the final fulfillment of the interpersonal relationship of sexual love and dedication in marriage, the young seminarian could hardly be expected to make the personally binding commitment of his own sexual function into the hands of Christ as an act of joyful, fruitful, and self-fulfilling love. For him, unless he were unusually perceptive, or had good private counseling, dedicated celibacy in the sense of this book would hardly be psychologically possible.

This double inadequacy in the two key areas which we have discussed reveals itself also in the spiritual formation given in many seminaries. The students' personal love of Christ is not directed towards the gradual and responsible development of a commitment involving the deep center of his person and the whole developing function of his manhood. Its direction is rather that of a pious approach to Christ in the Eucharist, and in the Sacrament reserved on the altar; this is often not devotion in its true sense of being vowed or dedicated to a person but rather a complex of pious feelings and aspirations engendered by sermons and meditations, many of which would be regarded as oversentimental in a girls' high school. These tend to produce in those seminarians who are unable to think their own way through their religious development, a rather pietistic approach to spirituality. This approach is equally removed from the hard challenge of the Gospels and from the realities and conflicts of daily life, realities from which the seminarian is all too often shielded. This kind of spiritual formation has a deep influence on the common life of the Church in its parishes, and is being pointed to with despairing accuracy by many lay writers of our day.

All of these factors go to make up a rather depressing picture—inadequate psychology, a theology developed often enough on the basis of unreality, poor student involvement in learning and training, a formation in areas of decision which seems often to be a training for irresponsibility, an overemphasis of authority both in learning and in the observance of the small rules borrowed from monastic living—all of these tend to make the seminary a very unreal place for the growth and development of a young twentieth-century man. The "outside world" is shut out by the high walls, mental as well as physical, of the average seminary. The misplaced emphasis on the values of solitude, silence, detachment from the things of this world, tend to produce very often a rather priggish, withdrawn, irrelevant young scholastic to bring God's message to the people of today.

Pius XII felt it necessary, in his letter of 1950, to refer openly to this deficiency:

When young men have been educated, especially from their tender years, in places somewhat too secluded from normal social intercourse, they will find some difficulty afterwards in adjusting themselves to the ways not only of the educated, but also of the ordinary people. Commonly such men will be either thoughtless in their behavior or will come to take a disparaging view of the education they have received. Care, therefore, should be taken so that the students are gradually and prudently introduced to a knowledge of the sentiments and outlook of the general public. They will not then suffer from indecision in their priestly work, causing them distress and diminishing their efficiency.

At least I and many priests of my acquaintance can find some consolation in the fact that the Pope recognized that many of us would come to have a disparaging view of the education we have received.

IMPORTANCE OF TRAINED COUNSELORS
IN SEMINARIES

The Pope's recognition of the danger that young priests trained in this traditional type of seminary will suffer from indecision leads us to a further major inadequacy of the seminary which has a large effect in the quality of commitment possible at the subdiaconate. Very few seminaries seem to have paid much attention to providing mature and trained counselors for their students. All seminaries have what is usually called a spiritual director, a priest often chosen for his personal holiness, devotion, and prudence, rather than for his manliness, his maturity, his training and experience in the field of counseling. He is regarded as a spiritual guide and personal consultant for the students. The very name director gives an indication that this guidance is usually based on the old attitude that one man can be responsible for the free and conscientious decisions of another; and this is the way it very often works in practice.

The spiritual director, often enough an elderly man, must work within the seminary system. He aims generally at an individualistic and legalistic kind of holiness and devotion in his students rather than the kind of mature and love-inspired responsibility necessary if celibacy is to be a deeply felt decision. Spiritual directors are very prone to declare "the will of God" to a student who is somewhat doubtful at the time of subdiaconate as to whether he should go on or not. It is a common thing for students at this stage to become rather hesitant and doubtful. They are, after all, young men in their early twenties who have been subjected to some years of training in submissiveness and "self-forgetfulness." Their hesitation is to some extent a natural human reaction, but sometimes it represents a real indecision; often enough a spiritual director, completely untrained in psychology and counseling, will be familiar with the pleasant personal qualities of the student and will consider that he has all the makings of a good and holy priest; he will urge him on by telling him that this step into celibacy is the will of God for him. This human presumption, this tendency to play the part of God in someone else's life, is one of the real temptations in the life of any priest.

It is sadly common for priests in their later years, troubled by their lack of commitment to the law of celibacy, to tell of the real doubts they went through before the subdiaconate, and the way in which they were encouraged to go on by a kindly old spiritual director. There is surely no room in the Christian life for anyone who wants to be a "director of souls." The only one who might carry out this function is the Holy Spirit of love; but he works always in the ways of love, asking us for whatever love we are freely capable of giving in return. In human terms, he is completely non-directive in all areas where no law or obligation is at stake.

One of the most solid conclusions of modern psychology is that the counseling of others in their major life-decisions can be most harmful unless it is firmly based on the client's total involvement in the forming of his own free decision. If there is ever a proper field for non-directive counseling, it is surely that of guiding another human being in the making of a permanent sexual commitment, whether in marriage, the religious life, or priestly celibacy. Just as I would not, as a counselor, presume to direct anyone on their decision about marriage, so I would be horrified at the thought of spiritually directing a young man into celibacy.

If the celibacy of the priest is to have the kind of renewal we have considered, the most urgent reforms are needed in the whole field of preparation for the priesthood. These reforms demand serious changes in the staffing, curriculum, aims and spirit of seminaries. Some of these have already been suggested. In the last chapter we saw some suggestions for the breaking up of the long years of enclosed monastic, academic formation with intervening periods of practical work and experience under the supervision and tutoring of selected priests. Flowing from this must come major changes in the seminary curriculum to meet the practical needs of these working periods. The old static forms of Scholastic philosophy and theology must evolve towards a training designed to meet the intellectual needs of a priest in the modern Church.

In the early part of the seminarian's training, his studies should center around God, man as individual and in society, and the task of the Church in bringing God's message to the man of today. The indications are already evident, in the Vatican Council's Constitution on the Liturgy, of a new approach to the teaching of theology through salvation history and the whole of Scripture, and through the living liturgy of the worshipping community. This first period of training should be a vital introduction for the student, as he studies the dynamism of God's loving action among men. He should study the whole story of God's revelation to men through the salvation-events at the center of man's history, through the written form of his Word in Scripture, in the living person of the Word in Christ, and in the community life of the Church. The first seminary period, lasting three or four years, should show the Holy Trinity, the Scripture and the living Church to the student in such a way that he has, when he goes out for his first official apostolate as a catechist, a true and genuine message to give to men.

In order to do this, he must also study men. While there is much to be learned from the ancient disciplines of philosophy, especially when they are brought to life in history and made relevant to man's deep needs and aspirations, there is equally much to learn from the modern studies of man as individual and in society. All the branches of modern psychology—child development and maturation, educational psychology, social psychology, social casework, individual and group counseling, abnormal psychology, the non-directive approach to human problems—all of these should be dealt with, at least at the introductory level. Through the insights and techniques of sociology, a close study should be made of the way men live in society, particularly in the type of society in which the student is to work as a catechist. The other subjects studied during this first period of seminary training should be stamped with the same vital approach.

Pius XII pointed out, in his letter of 1950, that

in literary and scientific studies the future priest should not yield place to laymen who are taking the same course. If this standard is adopted, the mind of the clerical student will be more thoroughly trained, and the choice of candidates for ordination will also be made easier. The student will feel completely free to make up his own mind and he will run no risk, through lack of the necessary education for a lay career, of being constrained to follow a course not marked out for him.

This is a clear indication that the intellectual formation of the seminarian in these first years after high school should be at the college and university level. In his training in psychology, social work and sociology, he should come up to the standard necessary for ordinary professional competence in these fields, and should gain the university degree usual in his country for one of his age. While not all candidates for the priesthood might be capable of advanced and specialized university work, it is difficult to see that a man should be accepted in ordinary circumstances for work in the ministry if he is not capable of rising to the level of intellectual competence necessary to be a schoolteacher or social worker. He should have at least a modest competence in all these allied studies, and in the techniques of helping other human beings, instructing and guiding them. Those of the students who show the ability and capacity for further university work should be encouraged to do postgraduate work to the full extent of their ability, so that they meet those engaged in intellectual work in their society on a level of equality.

If the intellectual training of the candidate for orders is to be at the college and university level, the seminary should no longer be regarded as a closed institution intellectually, but should be integrated in some way with the ordinary university studies of the country. Many of the seminary courses will continue to be special to its own aims, but wherever possible the courses should be integrated with those of a university for the gaining of degrees. The ideal would be that the seminary is regarded as a specialized hall of residence within or adjacent to a large university. This would facilitate the interflow of ideas most useful for both the staff and students of the seminary, and would ensure the maintenance of normal intellectual standards.

The Church in its history has used basically three institutions for the formation and training of its ordained ministers, the cathedral, the university, and the monastery. In the early centuries the students were trained around the bishop in his cathedral, and gradually came largely to receive most of their training under the supervision of priests in parishes. During the Middle Ages, insofar as any serious training was given to priests, it was generally in the universities. In reaction against the Reformation, the Church turned to the monastic model for the setting up of seminaries. In the circumstances of the time, seclusion from the world, and seclusion from worldly ideas and influences were regarded as prime essentials for the training of secular priests who would be models of virtue and learning. While this seminary system has had undoubted success in achieving some of its rather limited aims, it played a large part in helping to form the great void between the priest and the people he was to serve, a void very noticeable during the nineteenth century and increasingly evident today.

The task of today is to find a synthesis of the three traditional approaches to the training of secular priests. The priest should be familiar with the best of current thought on man and his problems through the university studies he does in common with the other professional people of his society; he will receive from the parish, during his practical periods of apostolate, a vital contact with the community life of the Church under the advice and guidance of selected priests; in his periods in the seminary proper he will gain the benefit of the silence, seclusion, and prayerful atmosphere to enable him to assimilate the fruit of his outside experience. It is out of the learning of life that he will absorb in his university work and in his periods of pastoral work as catechist and as deacon, that he will gain the experience to be the basis of realism for his more specialized studies and his seminary formation.

Throughout the whole of the student's studies, he should receive the advantage of the best of modern techniques of education. For example, it is widely recognized that direct lecturing has a limited value in forming a responsible and inquiring mind; the more active, student-centered, better-motivated approach, through personal research involving reading, reporting, writing, discussions, seminars and practical projects, will help bring into the focus of life many of the subjects which, in most seminaries, are still in the realm of abstraction and essentialist theory.

SOME CONTEMPORARY EXPERIMENTS

A good deal of experiment in finding a new form for the training of priests has already begun, particularly in Europe. An interesting example in France involves the unification of six existing diocesan seminaries in one scheme of training in three stages. There will be a philosophy course of two years, a three-year theology course, and a year of pastoral work and study. At the pastoral seminary, the young priests will come together regularly during the first few years of their priesthood for further training. The bishops stated that they are aiming to provide the kind of priest that the present day requires. "We want to give these young priests . . . a training in the spirit of the gospel that will allow for the free development of their personality and enable them to perform within the Church their duties towards their brethren wholeheartedly and without reserve."[1]

From discussions during the third session of the Vatican Council in November, 1964, it is evident that the Church will rely very largely for seminary reform on the initiative of small groups of local bishops, as in the French example we have just seen. It is difficult to see that this could be otherwise in view of the widely differing circumstances in different countries. Cardinal Suenens made a notable contribution to the discussion, pointing out that present seminaries were based in some degree on religious houses, and may be unsuited for the training of secular clergy. He called for a reorganization of theological studies, for practical pastoral training in leadership, and for a pastoral emphasis throughout the whole cycle of training.[2] The Cardinal had previously, in a press conference, outlined the experiment going on in his own diocese, based on the results of a survey made among his own diocesan priests. These results had emphasized the fivefold isolation in the life of the priest— his difficulty in achieving union with God, the distance between himself and his bishop, between himself and other priests, his isolation from lay people, and his isolation from the world. The structure of the experimental seminary was designed to make living contact for the student in these five areas. The seminarians are trained from the beginning to go out to meet people, to be leaders in the lay apostolate. They

---

[1] "Seminary Centralization in France," in *Herder Correspondence*, October, 1963.
[2] *Catholic Herald*, London, November 20, 1964.

are trained in an active spirituality aimed equally at union with God and union with men, stressing not the mortification of withdrawal, but the mortification of the outward apostolate. The students live and work in teams, living a family life in groups of seven in separate houses, working and accepting responsibility as a group.[3]

It seems certain that the Vatican Council will state certain agreed principles of universal application in the training of priests, and leave it to local groups of bishops to make the practical experiments towards the new form of training suited to their own conditions and to the needs of the Church in their area. The experiments we have described give examples of the kind of adventurous thinking and reorganizing that will be required to make this policy fruitful in each local situation. It cannot be too strongly emphasized that the structure and form of seminary training is a key factor in a renewal of the whole area of the priest's life-dedication which is the subject of this book.

The staffing of the new seminaries, as they are established, or evolved out of the old institutions, will present a large problem. As Archbishop Colombo of Milan stated in the Council, "Good seminaries depend more on good men rather than on good laws."[4] Most present seminaries are staffed by priests who have, after their ordination to the priesthood, or even during their seminary course, done courses in theology, scripture or canon law in the theological colleges in Rome. While the degrees from these colleges provide them with a working basis of scholarly research in these fields, they are too often founded on a set of educational attitudes which would be regarded as inadequate and old-fashioned by the scholars of a modern university. Many universities do not regard the doctorate of philosophy granted in Rome as having real standing and importance in the world of modern

---

[3] *Catholic Herald,* London, November 6, 1964.
[4] *Catholic Herald,* London, November 20, 1964.

scholarship. While there are signs of real progress in the Roman colleges, it seems that low scholastic standards and outdated techniques still prevail in many of the ecclesiastical schools of higher learning, both in Rome and other centers. Those who are to staff the new seminaries should be adequately educated, not only in the better schools of modern theology and scripture, but also in the schools of education, psychology, social science, sociology, and history available in the better universities.

The staffing of the seminary is a key to the whole life-problem of the priest in the modern world, and to the kind of dedication of which he will be capable. The difficulties of the personal commitment of the priest in his celibacy are traceable not only to structure and aims in need of reform, but also to the kind of intellectual formation and personal training which he receives from the staff of the seminary. Those responsible for seminaries, then, should make their choice of staff with even greater care than is given to the choice of professors for a university. They should be able to range over the whole field of suitably educated priests in their country, and even, at times, those of other countries.

One of the great difficulties in doing this, is the present custom in many areas of entrusting the staffing of the local diocesan seminary to some relatively small religious order of priests. Inevitably, such a small group, often with widely flung activities, can only make a reasonable choice from its own men available; it could hardly be expected to be always able to provide the kind of highly selected and well-qualified staff demanded in the type of seminary just described. It matters little, in the choice of such a staff, whether a priest is a member of one religious order or another, or a member of the diocesan clergy; it is from all priests available that the best in terms of maturity, teaching ability, and intellectual attainment should be chosen for the staffing of such an important professional school.

Pius XII laid down the principle that seminarians should be educated at a level equal to that of other young men in training for professions. This means that a priest teaching in a seminary should have an intellectual capacity and appropriate degrees suitable to qualify him for a teaching position in a university. If this were so, it would make possible a real communication of ideas and research projects between seminary and university, and open up the further possibility of occasional interchange of lecturing staff. Thus, a priest lecturer at the seminary might teach for a period in the neighboring university, gaining for himself a wider view of teaching techniques, closer acquaintance with scholars in his field, and valuable contact with lay students.

A most important requirement for the staffing of the new kind of seminary, is a sufficient number of well-qualified and mature student counselors. These should be priests with full training and experience in psychology and social work, and knowledge of the modern techniques of casework and counseling. A seminary rector would not dream of providing medical advice for his students from some person who was not qualified in medicine, so he should not provide counseling except from one who is properly qualified. A trained priest will have a professional confidence and ability in dealing with the rather complex problems of growth and decision that normally arise in counseling students for the ministry, especially as they approach the major decisions which are to give form and commitment to the whole of their adult lives.

Finally, it should be regarded as a normal thing that on the staff of a seminary there should be suitably qualified lay people, both men and women. It is not to be expected that in any country all the best-qualified people for the training of priests will be themselves priests. Some might be deacons, some might be catechists, and, surely, some of them might be lay men and women. They will be able to bring into the hitherto closed world of the seminary their own experience of the reality of Catholic living in their families, their parishes, and in the whole society of the country. The only really important requirements in the selection of a seminary staff are personal maturity, religious development, and intellectual attainment, combined with teaching ability. It would be rash indeed for any one to judge that there are, in our Western societies at the moment, no lay people who measure up to these requirements.

Provision should also be made, as in universities, for visiting lecturers who will bring into the life of the seminary their varied experience, and the results of their study and research. Some of these visiting lecturers should certainly be parish priests, who will bring not only their experience and wisdom, but also the image of the actual working out of the problems of being a priest in the world today. As with the proposed interchange of staff with universities, there should also be an interchange of the seminary priest with the parish priest and curate, so that the priest who is to be spending most of his life as a seminary teacher will have practical periods of pastoral work for his own growth and experience.

THE SEMINARY OF TOMORROW

We begin to see emerging an ideal of the seminary of tomorrow, towards which the seminary of today should be developing. It is an institution which is much more open-minded and more openly-situated than is normal at present. It will be close to a good university, near also to large numbers of priests in their pastoral work who will meet often at the seminary to discuss with staff and students the pastoral implications of studies and training. It will be regarded in society, and in the university, as a specialized professional school at university level, with a standard and style of education readily acceptable by the intellectual and professional people of modern society. There will be a level of theoretical work and of social and religious research that commands respect in the intellectual community. The students will be given, in their periods of practical assignment and in their vacation periods, work to be done which will deepen their understanding of the society in which they live and of its need for Christ in the life of his Church. The value of these assignments will be evident to those who are familiar with modern schools of psychology, sociology, and social science.

Above all, tomorrow's seminary should be a place of formation with a new aim and spirit that corresponds to our ever-deepening understanding of the growth and development of man towards maturity. It will see as its main task the formation of men of maturity marked with a high sense of personal responsibility. Its aim will be to form in its students a large capacity for deeply-felt decision arising from that existential freedom which is one of the marks of full personal growth. This maturity, responsibility, and freedom form the necessary human base of the total commitment of the person in Christ which the celibacy-ideal of the priest demands. Gone from this seminary of tomorrow will be all those institutional forms which promote childish submissiveness, lack of responsibility and maturity, and lack of manliness.

The kind of seminary we picture will be a place where the students will take part in an authentic experience of Christian community life. Many seminaries are already working towards this through the liturgical life of the students; as the reform of the liturgy proceeds, the students should experience, in their common prayer with Christ, the true values of the Christian community. This in itself will be a corrective to much of the remoteness and isolation from community life and values which has been one of the problems of modern seminaries and of the life of priests.

Parish priests have often discussed with me the impression made on them by seminarians when they are home on vacation. In comparison with the active lay people of the parish, involved in their works of apostolate and community endeavor, the seminarian often appears to be a lifeless Christian. It appears almost as if his Christian life will not begin for him until the end of his seminary course, as if the seminary time is a period of non-involvement, of non-living. This is an area in which reform is already under way in many seminaries, but a great distance is yet to be covered. It is not sufficient, for the authentic Christian life and experience of a young man of twenty, that he collects stamps for the missions, or makes an occasional visit to a hospital or prison. His whole Christian life in all its aspects must be vigorously growing through and in the seminary training.

On the intellectual side there will be an open spirit of free inquiry, a continuing search on the part of staff and students for a deeper grasp of personally-held truth. This will be marked by a strong religious confidence on the part of the professors, lecturers, and counselors that such a search after truth, conducted with utter honesty and without bias of any kind, will end in Christ who is the unveiling to us by the Father of truth that is ultimate and infinite. There will be little room for the attitude, still common in seminary faculties, of trying to protect their students from the errors of modern scholars; they will present the world of today, including the intellectual world, as it really is, with all its doubts, indecisions and aimlessness, so that the student may see the world's need for Christ, and his own need for a firmly-structured faith if he is to bring to the world the message of Christ and his ministering love.

The new kind of seminary, because it is based on a deep understanding of man, of his origin, of his growth toward maturity, will find an ever-deeper meaning in the whole development of sexuality in man and woman. This will bring into focus the high degree of interpersonal love demanded of those who are to enter into marriage or into priestly celibacy. The student will gain the confidence that it is only in full human maturity that he can find the capacity for life dedication; he will realize that it is only in the growth of his love-drive to its full capacity in the warmhearted love between persons that a priest can find the power to so mold his life into the love of Christ that he becomes the ministering hands of divine love for a love-hungry world.

It would be unjust not to recognize that many seminaries for the diocesan priesthood, still a small proportion, have made a good beginning of the kind of renewal of their aims and spirit, their staffing, curriculum and style of education, along such experimental lines as are discussed here. All praise is due to those bishops and priests who are supplying the energy for these reforms. However, it seems that the majority of seminaries are, in varying degrees, culpable of many if not most of the faults outlined in this chapter. The energy, zeal, devotion and good will of staff and students of these schools are being largely wasted within a basically faulty system.

Most of the seminaries in which today's priests have been trained were not marked by the kind of confidence in man's true line of development, of which we have been speaking. There has been evidence of a kind of uneasy dualism, which tends to mark much Catholic work in the educational field. This ancient dualism, this division of man into body and soul, into material and spiritual, into "the things of this world" and those of the next, receives its full and ultimate denial in the Incarnation. However, it tends always to be creeping back into Christian thought and attitudes as if the full meaning of the penetration of the divine into human nature and human affairs is still beyond our practical belief. The coming of the Second Person of the Trinity as a real and complete man, bound men to himself in the love of the Spirit in such a way that their humanity is not belittled but fulfilled in the full power of its growth. This is the definitive answer to that divisiveness of matter and spirit, of body and soul, which is the great continuing heresy against Christian faith and practice.

The total dedication of the person of the priest in his celibacy-commitment should be a striking expression, and a living sign to the world of men, of this union of all that is fully human in the divine life of love. The divine life into which the celibate priest totally consecrates himself is not based on any denial of his humanity, but on its fullest potential for growth and development. That is why maturity, and responsibility in its ultimate sense, is the only basis on which the priest's celibacy can express its meaning. It is for this reason that our next regular chapter must deal with Christian maturity—raising the question as to whether there really is such a person as a man who is both fully mature and fully Christian in a unified line of growth, as to whether a priest, in making the loving of Christ the central, totally-absorbing energy and aim of his being, and leaving aside the potential of interpersonal love and dedication represented by a wife and family, is becoming to that extent less a man.

This, after all, is the common hidden image of the priest in the minds of most people, even of Catholics. It is a common experience of priests to note the air of discovery about the mature, well-educated man when he tells of meeting some priest who impressed him as having the manly qualities of full maturity, as if somehow this is hardly a thing one normally expects; he will sometimes add, as if by way of further compliment, that this man didn't seem like a priest at all. With Catholics, this hidden image of the priest, as one who has given up being human for the sake of the divine, is overlaid by a deep devotional respect for the function of the priesthood, and often by a warm personal regard for the kindly and affable qualities of the priests whom they know. In the case of most of the post-Christian men of our day, the priest is an odd person, a person who has made a dedication, however admirable, to things which are no longer relevant because they are no longer human; they see in the priest a sign of contradiction, not so much of the evil, pettiness and self-centeredness of men, but rather of the positive human values of growth, responsibility, and maturity which they hold dear.

The lives of the priests in the highly developed areas of the West, however admirable in their effort, have on the whole given some substance to this common view of their place in human affairs and strivings. Many of them show a lack of human integration and a general restlessness, anxiety, and frustration. This lack of inner purpose which seems to stem from the low quality of personal involvement in the dedication of their lives, is sensed by their fellowmen and transmuted into the tolerant image of irrelevance which we have seen. But it is not only on the practical side that the man of today does not see in the priest the full human value; it is not only because of their strangely cut-off lives and their somewhat narrow and individualistic attitudes; there remains a strong theoretical doubt in the minds of many modern men of serious thoughtfulness, a doubt that ultimately is about Christianity itself. Is Christianity truly a religion of maturity? Can any man, by becoming more deeply devoted and dedicated to Christ in his Church, be thereby achieving the fulfillment of his manhood?

8:

CAN A CELIBATE PRIEST BE A
TRULY MATURE MAN?

RECENTLY A FRIEND OF MINE asked me to explain to him what was meant and intended by the celibacy of priests. He was a lecturer in sociology in a state university, and asked me in particular what relevance celibacy could have for our local society. I told him of the complete commitment of the person that celibacy represented and of the fact that this personal dedication was to the love of Christ and all his people; it was meant to be as deep, permanent, and meaningful as a marriage bond. I emphasized that it was a consecration of the sexuality of a mature man with normal sexual development; that he freely chose to forego the fulfillment of sex in marriage in order to give it its highest possible meaning and function in a high dedication of love and service. It is this total dedication of love and service which is its relevance to our society—there is nothing more relevant to any society of men.

My friend admitted the relevance of dedicated love and remarked that this was the kind of thing that prompted some of his university friends to volunteer, at low salaries, for service in emerging countries. "At its best," he said, "this is a kind of high maturity for human beings, certainly when it is being done with really human motives. I can understand this in a humanist, but when a Christian does this sort of thing, it seems to be with mixed motives, in response to a demand from a heavenly father-figure who promises rewards. This seems to make it impossible for the dedication to be humanly mature." Our discussion turned to maturity, and he told me that he felt it as a kind of pleasant accident when he met a mature priest, because he considered that Christianity, which he had learned and practiced as a boy, was a religion of immaturity, really suitable for children and for adults who have failed to grow to their full emotional development. "Which is why," he concluded, "Christianity is so popular and so useful in society—most people don't ever mature to a very high degree, so they continue to need a father-religion to give them security, protection, and reward. Christianity answers very well to their deep psychological needs."

I told him, of course, that this was quite true, at least for many Christians, and he was encouraged to go on and explain. "Think of the Lord's Prayer," he said. "It is an act of submission to the will of your Father, the King of all creation, asking him for your daily needs and for protection from harm. Then Christ himself told you that you must become like little children to enter the Kingdom. It is summed up beautifully in his story of the prodigal son who comes back from his independence into his father's arms; most adults are basically insecure and lonely, afraid of their freedom, of their own evil and despair, so they must have a heavenly Father to come home to. They become the adopted children of their Father by the washing away of their evil in baptism. Then they must be submissively obedient to their Father's laws, so they live along somewhat anxiously and carefully, secure in the thought that this wins them protection, love, and final reward. In the struggle of life, they are on the right side forever. All this is fine for most people, but fails to have meaning for a mature man—he doesn't need this any more. Surely, after all his effort in attaining maturity, he is not going to surrender it completely into the hands of God and live simply as a little child of a heavenly Father? So," he concluded, "your celibacy is not mature at all; it is the utmost in childishness. Your real maturity comes from the humanist elements in your education; you are really leading a double life, with two contrasting value-systems—it must be quite a strain."

I replied to my friend that I would give him a high mark for his social psychology, but a low mark for theology—that he had given a clear picture of popular Christianity, of what he had heard as a child, and observed in the lives of practicing Christians; that his theory to explain why Christianity was popular seems to fit the facts of modern society as we know it. "The sad thing," I said, "is that this is not Christianity at all, it is just what you call it, a popular father-religion based on psychological need, and, often enough, its's quite childish. I can assure you that my dedication of celibacy is not based on this religion, but on the Christianity of the New Testament." Our discussion ended, for the time, by his taking home a copy of the New Testament and promising to talk to me again about my celibacy after he had finished reading it.

We may think it very sad that a trained social observer could report on the popular Christianity of our time as a father-religion, with no reference to the work of Jesus or the Holy Spirit, that he should see Christians not as people energized by divine love but only as men and women seeking, out of their loneliness and anxiety, for security, protection, and rewarding love. It leaves us with the conclusion that the dedicated humanists of our time have merely been rejecting a false religion, and quite rightly; that they have not yet heard of true Christianity, nor, on the whole, have they seen much of it. This is true not merely of a few university scholars—it seems to be true of some large proportion of the well-educated people of our Western societies.

A great number of the intellectuals of our society seem to be alienated people. In becoming alienated from God, they have gradually lost touch also with reason and with the meaning of man. Their reality is a reality only of personal experience, of what exists for them. Since they have lost their experience of God, he is nonexistent for them, and no argument of faith or reason reaches them. This is why, for them, the witness of the priest is more important than his theories —this is the only way he can reach into their personal experience. They tell a story of a Communist in the Peace Corps remarking, "I'm not interested in what the Christians believe, I just want to know where they are."

But before the witness of the priest in his celibacy is experienced, he must be recognized as a man. Men must feel him to be truly human before they will look at what he has of the divine. He must give to the modern man the experience of seeing in him a consecration to all the high human values of maturity before they will suspect that there might be something in his celibacy. To meet the sad emptiness of much of modern thought, the priest must bring his experience of being fully human and at the same time fully Christian, filled with the hope and joy of the Resurrection. This presents us with a very serious challenge of finding out for ourselves the vital relationship between the maturity of a man and the message of Jesus in the Church. It is this relationship which is the basic theme of this book, for without it the celibacy of the priest is meaningless.

The life-commitment of the true Christian is not to any protective father-figure created out of his loneliness and anxiety, but to the Father through the Son in the Holy Spirit; his Baptism is in the name of all three persons and his dedication is in all three. It is by taking this step of faith in the revelation of the three, made in the divine salvation-events of history, presented in the Scripture, and in the living community of the Church, that a man becomes a Christian. By freely stepping into this complex of persons, events and energies, a man commits himself into a realm of growth, of dynamic development, of love-energy, which is the very opposite of the popular father-religion seen by the sociologist. It was because de Chardin was able to express to his fellow scientists this view of Christianity in terms of the dynamic energy of creative love that he is regarded by many as the only intelligible Christian of our time.

When the modern humanist tries to define his commitment to the ideal of man's emerging growth and development, he generally speaks of three things—man's totally-dedicated search for truth; his social quest for peace, interpersonal service and love; and his striving for identity and self-meaning, for personal fulfillment and security. It is no accident that this basic search and dedication to human values is a reflection of the revelation of the Trinity of divine Persons, of the Son who is the truth-image of all reality, of the Spirit who is the dynamism of interpersonal love, and the Father who is origin and fulfillment. We have seen earlier that the total dedication of marriage and of celibacy show, for the Christian, sacramental images of the divine love for man; the natural strivings of modern man towards truth, growth, and peace, are equally an image of the triple divine reality which is man's origin and destiny.

As we watch God's message to man gradually unfold in the New Testament we begin to see the great revelation that the redeemed men of the new human race are to live within the vitality of the Trinity, and, within this relationship to the three Persons, find the fulfillment of their growth potential. Jesus uses sacramental symbols of water, food, and drink, the necessities of human life and growth. He gives us a picture of himself as a growing vine planted by his Father, and tells us that we are the branches and twigs of this vine, living and growing by the same life, which is the love he has received from the Father and is giving to us. We must live on his love, learning to love one another as he has loved us. He speaks of the Spirit who will come to live within our being as the energizing force of truth and love.

St. Paul speaks of Christ as the new Adam, the first of the new race of redeemed and liberated men, marked by the maturity of manhood fulfilled and perfected: "So we shall reach perfect manhood, that maturity which is proportioned to the completed growth of Christ; we are no longer to be children . . . we are to follow the truth in a spirit of charity, and so grow up, in everything, into a due proportion with Christ who is our head." (Epistle to the Ephesians, c.4.) St. Paul sees man before Christ's coming as bound in a captivity of infantile self-centeredness; Christ's redeeming act was for men a radical liberation from self by the love of the Spirit, by which we are able, with Christ, to approach the Father as sons. Time and again St. Paul stresses this vital rebirth of the Christian within the dynamic relationships of the three Persons, emphasizing that this establishes man in an attitude, not of dependent childishness, but of free sonship with a divine right of inheritance.

It is only as free and mature adopted sons that we are children of the Father; it is only because he has sent his Spirit of love to dwell in our being that we are able to call him Father. It is the ultimately mature interpersonal love, the love of the Son for the Father, speaking in us, not any mere anxious cry of a lonely child for a father's protection. While this existential human loneliness, anxiety, and awe remain part of us, it is swept up, enriched, and matured by the Spirit of Jesus dwelling in the inner center of our being, transforming us into sons of heaven and princes of the Father's kingdom of all reality. The Lord's Prayer, which, humanly considered, seems to reflect a childish view, takes on a new maturity and a grown-up demand, when we join with Jesus in saying it, in a spirit of mature love. This prayer is Christian only when we say it within Jesus, in his

Spirit. This is the sense in which a mature man is born again and becomes like a child; for the way into the final reality of the Trinity is the way of Jesus, of being united vitally with him in complete dedication and loving service. It is the way of love without limit. It is only by responding to this loving demand of a new adulthood, in the self-liberation of union with Christ, that we are able to come to the Father's welcoming arms.

Marx described the popular Christianity which he saw in his time as an opiate for the people. Freud referred to it as a universal obsessional neurosis. There is a truth in these criticisms which we have too long ignored. Every neurosis is a kind of private religion divorced from any basis of reality. There is a wide tendency for Christians to halt their reading of the New Testament at the sermon on the mount, and to fashion for themselves a kind of spiritual opiate to deaden the pain of their own inadequacy and immaturity, to see religion as a kind of fire insurance, an after-death social security scheme. They ignore Christianity's true demand of mature love; they retreat from the challenge of dedicated service within their existential relationships with the three Persons of the divinity.

This highlights the tragedy of the low-level dedication of priests and their fairly general failure to live out in the practice of their lives the high ideal represented in their celibacy. It puts into hard focus the inadequacies we have seen in the whole present scheme and aims of training for the Church's ministry. It presents the whole community of the Church with a challenge to investigate and discuss the question of this chapter—is dedicated celibacy in a priest really compatible with his maturity as a man? Is it a feasible force of growth towards full and responsible manhood? Or does it leave a priest as a man of inner contradiction, not the elemental sign of contradiction between good and evil foretold of Christ, but the contradiction of inner disintegration in a man trying to live by two opposing systems of values?

Maturity, and the maturation process through childhood, adolescence, and adulthood, has been a fascinating field of exploration for modern psychologists since the early theorists opened up for discussion the basic drives, instincts, dynamisms, and conflicts of human growth. Many recent attempts have been made to integrate the results of this long discussion, notably by L. J. Saul in his book, *Emotional Maturity* (Philadelphia: Lippincott, 1947), and by E. H. Erikson in his work, *Childhood and Society* (New York: Norton, 1950). The leading ideas on human life-aims which are coming out of this work have a pointed relevance to our present question.

Maturity, the end of human growth, must have as its basis within ourselves a high degree of inner personal integration, forming a well-balanced and creative unity out of the growth of the various drives and energies of our being. The dynamisms of aggressiveness, of hostility, or sexuality, must grow beyond the stages of child and adolescent disunity to the point where they present a combined energy at the service of the person for positive and creative ends. For this to happen, the various inner forces of self-control must be developed and objectivized to be not merely a restraining force for coping with reality-demands but also a positive energy of the person directed towards what is responsible and productive.

In our relations with others, maturation is marked by the gradual development, from infancy to adulthood, of emotional independence from the parents and parent-figures, up to a point of grown-up self-reliance. This process is based on a growing sense of one's own identity, reality, and value as a person, both for oneself and for others, and a growing confidence that this meaning is consistent and worthwhile. A corresponding freedom from inferiority feelings, egotism, and undue competitiveness is a result of this inner growth. This development leads finally to a mature capacity for warm and lasting relationships that are truly interpersonal and are marked by an easy ability to receive and to give with equal grace, satisfaction and joy.

The grown-up personality is based on a firm sense of reality and an emotional acceptance of the real world-as-it-is. This grasp on reality is characterized by adaptability and flexibility of approach and by freedom from childhood fixations and fantasies. Through growth in these qualities the adult is liberated from the unreal, daydream worlds of fear, of hatred, of grandeur, of obsessive guilt-feeling, which create so much insecurity, inferiority, anxiety, and loneliness.

In short, our naturally mature man is, in his inner person, well-integrated, and is confident in the possession of his own worthwhile meaning and identity. He is responsible, warmhearted, and well-balanced in his dealings with others, and he is realistic in his grasp of reality. It is easy to see the link between these qualities of maturity and the triple demand of love made by Jesus, that we should love the Lord God with our whole being, and love others as we love ourselves. What is not so evident is that without the base of these human qualities of maturity, the Christian love of the Gospels, elaborated in the writings of St. Paul and St. John, very easily becomes in us a sham and a delusion.

For without the well-integrated growth of the human self, there is no basis for true self-esteem and self-love; without some measure of responsible and warmhearted emotional development towards others, there is no base in us for Christ's love of others to rest on. Without a firm and secure grasp and love for all that is real, there is no ground of true love for the center and source of all reality. Without this deep aliveness to reality, a Christian does not hear the true voice of the Father in the message of Christ. He will tend rather to choose some of the suitable Christian material of the Gospels and fashion the private religion of his own fantasies and inadequacies.

This seems to lead to the answer to our question. Not only is genuine Christianity compatible with human maturity, but it is its completion and fulfillment. Moreover, it is only as a person grows into human maturity that he becomes capable of being fully Christian; the quality of his Christian commitment to love will depend on the level of his personal growth and fulfillment, on the extent to which he has grown to be capable of mature interpersonal love. This clears priestly celibacy of the suspicion that, because it is totally Christian, it is, of itself, totally infantile and immature. But it presents it as a different kind of challenge. If what we have seen of the relation between true Christianity and maturity is true, it means that the total Christian consecration of the priest in celibacy can only be meaningful within a framework of a high level of personal maturity.

We have seen in previous chapters some of the practical reasons for this in terms of the philosophy of sexuality; this final theoretical synthesis presents an even more stern demand. The failure of a priest to find in his celibacy an integration of his growth as a man will lead him into a kind of false and private religion. He may still keep true to his external dedication of Baptism, and of priestly consecration in celibacy, but inwardly his life-view will not be that of the New Testament but that of a private contradiction and distortion.

SOME DIFFICULTIES

To say, as we have done, that it is only as a person grows into his human maturity that he becomes capable of being fully Christian, leads us into a twofold difficulty. The first side of this difficulty is shown in the remark of a friend of mine, after reading this, that my emphasis on the maturation process suggests a Stoic view of life rather than a Christian one. The wise man of the Stoics is self-sufficient, growing by his own effort into full development by a conscious conformity with himself and with the whole of nature. The other side of the difficulty, he suggested, is that this emphasis on maturity as the way to the Christian commitment of love seems to leave out the fact that the kingdom of Christ belongs to the lowly, the poor, the humble, those who by dying to themselves accept the new life of the risen Christ, something not their own making, but a free gift of the Spirit.

The area between psychology and theology is full of these challenging difficulties, forcing us into a deeper consideration of the leading ideas of each discipline so that we can arrive at a synthesis. This apparent conflict between the totality of our own effort at growth and self-fulfillment, and the total dependence we have on God and his gift of divine life, is nothing new. Spiritual writers of a former time were generally content to advise an "as if" attitude as a solution, like "work as if everything depended on yourself, and pray as if everything depended on God." This kind of advice, while practical, begs the question and is equivalent to saying that thinking of these problems is a waste of time.

There is a wealth of meaning in the promise of the beatitudes that "the meek shall possess the land." This is a quotation from Psalm 36, v.11, where the meek, the *anawim*, are promised that they will possess the land and enjoy abundant peace. *Anawim* is hard to turn into English; modern translators reject the colorless word "meek" in favor of "those of a gentle spirit," "the patient," "those who claim nothing," "the gentle." The basic idea seems to be embodied in those men who bend down before God in an attitude of self-surrender. We see the perfect fulfillment of this idea in the *Magnificat,* and in the self-description of Jesus as "meek and humble of heart." This total self-giving in face of the reality of God reflects itself in relation to the whole of nature and other men as patience and gentleness.

Psychology, as we have seen, leads us also to a point of self-surrender in face of reality, particularly in the inter-personal relationship of mature people. This is expressed and symbolized in the image of a well-integrated marriage relationship. The total acceptance of the reality of the other person, not in a false image distorted by any projection of our own need, but as fully existing in his or her own right, involves a surrender of our own selves to the other. This is ideally expressed in the joy-giving self-donation of sexual union with the beloved partner, in which it is only by giving all that we receive all—total possession of the other is only possible in the total giving of ourselves. This self-giving is possible only to the extent that we have grown to a degree of self-possession which substantially transcends the tensions and conflicts of childhood and adolescence. The compulsive seeking of satisfaction for self must give way to a really per-sonal attitude of complete acceptance of the other in the giving of oneself. This attitude of mature self-surrender and personal knowing of the other seems to be the natural basis on which our attitude to the supernatural reality of God will grow and develop.

It is, ideally, our knowing of Jesus in love which leads us into the scriptural attitude of total self-surrender to the Father. Our acceptance of the gift of his Spirit of love de-mands total self-giving from us in return. This dialogue of love is, of course, progressive. We enter into it when we first receive the gift of the Spirit in Baptism; it is a process which goes on until it finds its final consummation in the ultimate surrender of our death which is, at the same time, our full entry into the final meaning of being in love. Our psycho-logical growth and self-development is, therefore, not an isolated thing pursued for itself. It is something far more—

it is our part in this dialogue of love. Our effort, our self-fulfillment are totally our own, and, at the same time, totally God's, precisely because this is a relationship of love. In the ideal love-relationship of marriage, the husband's love for his wife is something that is totally his because it is part of himself and of his growth as a man. It is also totally his wife's, because it is completely given to her, and because it has come into being only in answer to the love which she has offered to him.

So the whole of our effort to mature in our human development is our own, in the fullest sense of the desire by my humanist friend whose objection started off this chapter on the maturity of the celibate priest. It is also, for the Christian, fully and wholly God's, not only because it is our response in self-surrender to the gift of the Spirit of love within us, but also because it is this Love which is making us grow. My friend felt that because his self-development was so surely his own, he could not surrender it into the hands of the Father and become like a child again. If he could understand that God's only demand on us is the demand of love, he would see that our self-donation is the only mature answer to the infinite love which is the origin and fulfillment of all being.

A final part of our difficulty is that we might now seem to have a picture of Christianity the very opposite of the popular father-religion with which we started. Christianity might seem to be a religion suitable only for mature, well-balanced, realistic people—a corps of elite. The full Christian message seems to demand a response of love, of dedication, of self-perfection beyond the capacity of the majority of human beings as we know them, handicapped as they are by all kinds of faults and deficiencies in their emotional development. We have only to ask ourselves how many perfect Christians we have met.

To take this argument to its conclusion is to miss the

meaning of love. A man and a woman in mature love are not in love with an ideal human being, but with a real one; realism is an essential quality of their maturity. It is this quality which enables each to see in the other a real person, not an idealized projection of their own inadequacy. Because they are loving a real person, the faults and weaknesses of the other are very much part of their love. Their acceptance of this reality of the person gives a deeper, richer quality to their love.

It is one of the strongest elements of the Father's message to us, in the Scriptures, and in the person of Jesus, that he is the supreme realist. His love for men is such that he is ready to accept the slightest movement of real love from the worst of human beings. The criminal dying on the cross beside Jesus seemed to be offering little enough, as did the woman caught in the act of adultery; perhaps they were stunted people who, like the widow offering her little coin in the temple, were giving all that they had of love at the time. The important thing is that they, the Apostles with all their immaturity, and so many others who met Jesus, were accepted into the divine kingdom of love all the same. The message of God's love is for all men, the mature ones, and the immature. It is for the saints and for the unholy, for the sane and for the insane, for the well-balanced and for the neurotics. It is for all men because all men are sinners, because all have a deep need for love's liberation from all in them that is evil and petty and infantile. For all of them, it is a challenge to further growth in love—not only in the direct response of love to the Holy Spirit, but in love of themselves and of their fellowmen. For there is no limit to love; it is never possible to say that we have loved enough. We can go on and on into love, for we are going on into the very heart of reality.

Thus it is in the New Testament that the priest will find the final synthesis of all the elements of his self-growth in maturity and of his self-surrender in total dependence on the Father, the self-surrender that finds its focus in his dedication of celibacy. The priest will see in the person of Jesus the ultimately mature human being who fulfills in himself all the qualities of high maturity discussed in this chapter. He will see equally in him, giving form and dynamism to all his human qualities, the total personal surrender to the reality of his Father, and the complete self-giving love and service of other men. He will recognize in Jesus the completed example of his own beatitude proverb, that those who make their total self-surrender to reality in love, gentleness, and patience, come into the full possession of all that is.

It is because we must love what is real, and accept what is, that I have tried in this book to be realistic about priests and their celibacy. For the starting-point of growth and renewal, in institutions as well as in individuals, is a loving acceptance of the real situation of the present. There is no opportunity for growth towards maturity while our present view is visionary, idealistic, and unreal. For the same reason, in outlining practical proposals for renewal in the priest's life-dedication, it was necessary to relate these proposals closely to the present situation within the Church. They were meant to be proposals for present consideration, taking into account the well-known difficulties of the situation of the moment, and the tendencies already present, such as the proposed revival of the diaconate, which lend feasibility to the postponing of priestly ordination to a much later age. The later age of making the celibacy-commitment, linked with a wide-ranging reform of training for the ministry, would tend to ensure that those who came freely to offer themselves to Christ and the Church in celibacy would be doing so with the mature capacity to make this commitment meaningful throughout the remainder of their lives.

For the lives of priests to be meaningful in these terms, there must be in them a deep personal integration of the religious and human values involved. They must be deeply committed to the idea of a constant striving for growth in union with Christ, a development within them of the energizing love of the Spirit, their lives oriented to the Father and marked with the high princely qualities proper to royal sons of the world. And it must be precisely within this religious framework, not alongside it or despite it, that the qualities of human maturity must be growing and flourishing. This must be particularly true in regard to the fulfillment of their own sexuality as men. Those characteristics of growth for the person which are possible for a husband in the sexual relationship of marriage must be fulfilled in the priest through his sexual consecration in celibacy. Through it, therefore, he must grow in dedicated self-donation and self-surrender, in the total commitment of himself in loving-service to the other, and in liberation from infantile self-centeredness and egotism. If celibacy cannot perform this function of sexual fulfillment for his manhood, it cannot relate him to Christ in the Holy Spirit in a service of love for the Church.

It is precisely on this ground that the argument has most often been put to me, by Catholic lay people and priests, that celibacy should no longer be a law, but should be left completely as a matter of free personal choice of the priest, whether before or after ordination. It is argued that this law had some prospect of functioning reasonably well in the life of the Church when little was understood of human maturation and the importance of sexuality, when the corresponding theology of marriage and Christian attitudes towards marriage were undeveloped. It can no longer be regarded as suitable for the present-day priest. It is pointed out that young men subject to religious fervor and enthusiasm may easily convince themselves that they are psychologically capable of sustaining such a dedication. However, with the increasing self-knowledge and self-awareness of early middle age, and the waning of fervor and enthusiasm, they are likely to find that the consecration of themselves made sincerely enough at an earlier time seems no longer to be valid and fruitful in terms of love and growth. The priest is faced with the same difficulty as a married man, but has not the intimate human relationship and normal sexual fulfillment to help him overcome the difficulty. It is only too common that, while clinging firmly to what remains of his religious dedication to Christ, he lapses, at the human level, into a sad loneliness and stagnation.

Those who have argued thus have agreed with the central theme of this chapter, that it is possible for a priest to find in his dedication of celibacy a fulfillment of his manhood, of the whole growing of his human nature, in an expression of love and service. They contend, however, that this is possible only in the framework of a deeply personal choice which must continue in freedom throughout the life of a priest; that every element of strictly-applied law should be removed from this personal consecration, so that consideration may be given to the changing circumstances of life, as the Church already does in releasing religious brothers from their celibacy.

As stated before, the practical suggestions of this book begin with the Church as it is, and with the priesthood as it is. As to whether the above argument would be verified in the modified arrangements which I consider feasible for the present, only time could finally tell. However, while time is passing, there is the opportunity for further discussion, open argument, and social research in those aspects of our question which are open to objective verification.

9:

THE PRIEST IN HIS CRISES OF GROWTH

IT IS IMPORTANT, at this stage, to gather together and to
deepen the ideas we have so far seen on the psychological
growth of the priest. All developmental psychology suffers
in the writing; it is necessary to generalize what is of its
nature personal and particular. To describe in general terms
the typical development of the priest is like the task of an
artist who tries with a few broad sweeps of his brush to create a vivid impression of a scene rather than present it pho-
tographically. What I have to say, therefore, is not expected
to be true of this priest or that; it is rather an attempt to
portray a general picture which will be substantially true of
the whole body of priests in the well-developed Western
societies. Because they are men of their own time and place,
the general conclusions of developmental psychology will
apply to them as well as to the men in their congregations;
there are, as well, certain characteristics of development
which stem from their dedication of celibacy, from their
training, and from their whole style of life.

It is understandable that comparatively little attention
has so far been given by psychologists to the subject of religious vocation; an outstanding exception is Erik H. Erikson's study of the early life of Luther (*Young Man Luther*),
to which reference will be made. I have already suggested

that the initial choice of a religious vocation involving celibacy could well be the subject of large-scale social research; it is of equal importance, as initial counseling at the preseminary stage and in the early seminary years takes on a more professional character, to have available some case studies in depth, to illustrate the dynamisms at the emotional level which may play a large part in the initial decision towards the celibate priesthood.

A priest in early middle age who was reading the script of this book had already discussed his own case with me at length; he suggested to me that his experience was a useful example of what I had been writing. Let us call him Father Andrew. Andrew, like his namesake the apostle, lived in the shadow of the limelight on his brother. He was one of five children, coming two years after his brother, the eldest of the family. Andrew has had throughout his life a great admiration of his brother, and a deep affection for him. He described him as well above average in intelligence, successful in athletics, and more than usually popular. It was only in the process of counseling in the area of his present problems that Andrew began to see how his own development and life-aims had been colored by the effect of his living as a child in the shadow of his clever, pleasant, and popular brother. He was able to recall how his parents had always set his brother before him as an example when he misbehaved or was careless about his schoolwork; his brother was unfailingly kind and generous with him, but their relationship was often marred by his own moodiness and temper tantrums. As he came into adolescence he was fired by the ambition to do better than his brother, at least in something.

It is easy for us to see, as Andrew has now come to see, that his adolescent ambition to be a priest had a natural emotional basis in this striving to better his brother's record of achievement. The important thing to note is that Father

Andrew came to see this himself only about the age of forty, when some minor symptoms of obvious psychic origin led him to seek some aid from counseling. He has come to realize that his present anxious perfectionism and compulsive drive to excel other priests can be related not only to his childhood experience, but also to the whole emotional basis of his decision to become a priest. He is slowly coming to see, also, that this is only part of a story in which other dynamisms of equal force, both natural and spiritual, have also played their part, and that these might play an increasingly important part in the shaping of his later life.

Even such a brief outline of a rather simple and ordinary case can help us see the type of problem which a trained counselor might be dealing with in the area of the initial decision concerning the priesthood in late adolescence. The problem of identity formation and of individuation in this period of early manhood are fully dealt with in psychological literature; a great deal of study is needed to determine the ways in which these natural processes play their part in the decision of a young man to become a priest and to dedicate his life in celibacy. Erikson, in his study of Luther, comments on the stresses of this period and their influence on the choice of life-commitment:

The one most exposed to the problem of his existential identity is the late adolescent . . . The introspective late adolescent, trying to free himself from parents who made and partially determined him, and trying also to face membership in wider institutions which he has not as yet made his own, often has a hard time convincing himself that he has *chosen* his past and is the chooser of his future. Moved by his ravenous sexuality, his commanding aggressive power, and his encompassing intellect, he is tempted to make premature choices, or to drift passively . . . When he must make many choices, as he does in our society, they may provoke a false sense of freedom, of indefinite time in which to experiment, and thus lead to moments in which it becomes suddenly clear to him that even in playing around he has been typed, and in trying things out, become committed to them.[1]

We have seen something of the uncertainty and doubt which afflicts many seminarians as they approach the point of final decision about celibacy before receiving the order of subdiaconate; we have suggested that because of the degree of maturity necessary to make this decision fruitful in terms of personal integration, dedicated love and interpersonal service, this final decision should be approached at a much later age. It is interesting to note that Erikson endorses Luther's opinion that the final decision on the monastic vocation should be postponed until thirty years of age, on the ground that true monasticism is a late development and is possible only to a mature ego. To the extent that a monastic type of training is retained for the formation of secular priests, it should be realized that this inwardly-oriented training brings difficulty as well as value to the maturing process of a young man. Erikson comments that

the monastery offers methods of making a meditative descent into the inner shafts of mental existence, from which the aspirant emerges with the gold of faith or with gems of wisdom. These shafts, however, are psychological as well as meditative; they lead not only into the depths of adult inner experience, but also downward into our more primitive layers, and backward into our infantile beginnings.[2]

To the extent that the modern seminary still retains so much of the monastic style of life and spirituality, one wonders whether it is really oriented towards the formation of secular

---

[1] Erik H. Erikson, *Young Man Luther,* New York: W. W. Norton, 1958, p. 109. (Italics are Erikson's.)
[2] *Ibid.,* p. 105.

priests who are to work as active apostles in the world. It is interesting to note that the small-group formation with relevant activity which Jesus used for his apostles is the subject of a new experiment by Cardinal Suenens.

In the present style of seminary formation, with a final decision on celibacy in the early twenties, it seems inevitable that the young priest will, if he is maturing normally, face another period of crisis in his psychological development around the age of thirty. After a few years of life as a priest, the attraction of novelty has passed away from the exercise of his high functions; the excitement of older people coming to him for mature advice has become a commonplace. He is then, often enough about five years after his ordination, left face to face with his priesthood itself and with the stern demand of personal dedication which it implies. If, as we have seen happen in many cases, the young man has begun his life in the priesthood with a low level of personal integration, and with a process of identity formation incomplete owing to a slow growth toward maturity, the problems of this early crisis of celibacy may well be intensified. Erikson, dealing with this period of Luther's life, comments on the tendency of young men to overcommit themselves to a variety of devotions and ideologies:

> They come to their crossroad, which they often do in their late twenties, belated just because they gave their all to the temporary subject of devotion. The crisis in such a young man's life may be reached exactly when he half-realizes that he is fatally overcommitted to what he is not.[3]

Willibald Demal, in his treatise on pastoral psychology, also advocates a later age for the celibacy decision, after a period away from the seminary. He comments on the kind of psychological crisis we have been describing:

[3] *Ibid.*, p. 40.

The psychic and biological characteristics of a young man at the age when he chooses his profession are essentially different from those of a man at the height of life between his thirtieth and fortieth year. Many a youth who cheerfully accepted the priesthood has had to suffer considerably later in life from the heroic sacrifice of celibacy and would gladly have renounced his former decision, had that been still possible. It has been urged by certain writers (e. g., Ruland) that a final decision concerning the priesthood should only be demanded at an age when the candidate is sufficiently mature to realize the consequence of his decision—and this maturity does not exist between the twentieth and twenty-fifth year of life.[4]

We have suggested that the undertaking of celibacy at the subdiaconate is often accepted by the young student as an inevitable legal step towards his real goal of the priesthood. If it has not been for him a mature and deeply free choice of an unusual form of life-dedication to the person of Christ and the service of his people in love, he may be left, about the age of thirty, with a vague sorrow and emptiness at the thought that he will never have a wife to stand with him as a source of joy, fulfillment, and strength in the struggle of life. He may feel keenly the urgency of sexual desire and of sexual loneliness as he sees his friends and relations choosing their life-partners with such joy and freedom, going off on their honeymoons, and establishing homes which seem so happy as centers of joy, companionship, and fulfillment. Although he may be very aware from his pastoral work and from marriage counseling that this ideal happiness is not achieved without tension, strain, and struggle, and is often marred by partial or complete failure in the growth of nuptial love, this means little in the context of his frustrated desires. His own unrest is woven from the material of a dream-image which admits none of the imperfections of the

[4] Willibald Demal, *Pastoral Psychology in Practice,* Cork: Mercier Press, 1950, pp. 184–185.

real world, but is more like the vague, unformed yearnings
of the adolescent.

CHALLENGES OF GROWTH

Many priests undoubtedly recognize this early crisis of their
priesthood as a challenge of growth, and rise through it to a
higher level of self-identity, of dedication, and integration.
Through it they find a deeper and more mature meaning for
their life-dedication in celibacy; they begin to see it not
merely as a convenient legal and social arrangement but as
a highly demanding form of personal consecration energized
by their love for Christ and his people. If they are able to
rise to this level, they may leave behind them many immature religious images and forms of spiritual devotion. Hopefully, they will find a solution of this growth crisis in a
steady development towards their Christ-image of total personal consecration and service. They will see in Jesus an
utter devotion of love to the point of death for the sake of
the other; by following him on this royal road, they will
experience the new life of the risen Lord as a free gift of
the Spirit of love.

The priest who develops in this direction will begin to
realize that it is precisely through this utter devotion of
loving service to others in Christ that his life is beginning
to find its final form and meaning. It is through this personal
consecration in the service of love that the true ideals of his
celibacy will find practical meaning and will become a dynamism of growth for his manhood. This gradual realization
is often accompanied by a reaction against the distortions of
monastic piety which have been, only too often, the staple
spiritual food offered in the seminary, in enclosed retreats,
and in literature on the priesthood. This piety offered as the
primary purpose of the priest's life the gaining of his own
salvation in heaven, achieved by a strenuous effort for self-

perfection through practices of prayer and virtue. His pastoral work as a priest was presented as a secondary aim to be achieved through growth in personal perfection, as something only possible and fruitful through the fulfillment of the first and dominant aim of his life. This kind of piety, borrowed with adaptation and distortion from monastic sources, was normally self-centered and introspective; it provided little help to the secular priest in meeting this crisis of active realization in the early years of his priesthood. It provided no energy to meet this crisis, this challenge to grow by rising to a higher level of integration and a more penetrating grasp of his own identity and life-aim.

The active holiness of the secular priest is not the holiness of the monk. It is the utter devotion of a dedicated messenger of love, not the withdrawn otherness of the contemplative. While both are equally forms of Christian love and dedication, the means they use and the expressions of love they aim at are vastly different. Every secular priest leading an active life of charity becomes conscious at some stage of the dichotomy between the urgent activity of Christ's love in him, and his deep need for reflection, for personal dialogue with Jesus, for loving interpersonal communion with the Spirit who is within him as the central source of his love-energy. The synthesis of this polarity in a meaningful style of life is the great task of maturity in the secular priest.

The formation commonly given in the closed type of seminary provides little help to him in this life task. The monastic kind of institution, with little or no active outlet of charity for the enthusiastic young student, inevitably teaches a one-sided spirituality. This results, all too often, in an uneasy dualism in the life of the priest which is furthered by the kind of literature in the priesthood normally available, and by enclosed retreats devoid of active orientation and usually conducted by priests who are themselves monks or religious. The demand made on the priest's life by active charity and evangelism comes to be regarded as an enemy of his "interior life." In this context, the priest's dedication in celibacy becomes self-centered and interiorized rather than the symbolic and dynamic expression of his active ministry of love and service. Activity, meeting people, entering into the commitment of apostolic endeavor, comes to be viewed as a danger to his celibacy rather than as its active fulfillment. In this frame of mind the priest may see no help except in further interior withdrawal when he comes to face the kind of emotional crisis which we have described as common in the early years of priesthood. If this early crisis period is not accepted as an opportunity for further growth in maturity, the priest will reach middle age poorly equipped to deal with its characteristic problems.

While most psychologists write a great deal about childhood and adolescence, few have much to say about mature adult life, especially in its later stages. Perhaps it is because so much of psychology is written for university students that many texts on developmental psychology give an impression that life ends about the age of twenty-five. A notable exception is Erikson, who follows the growth of the mature adult through the stages of later identity formation, generativity, and final integrity. Early middle age brings with it obvious developments in the psychology of women, linked with the menopause situation. What is not so obvious is a corresponding period of crisis development in the life of men as they come into middle age.

In the normal line of development, a man has apparently found himself by early middle age. He has chosen a wife, established a family, settled down to his vocational position and to his role in the community. In most cases the urgency of his striving is over, and his life-pace seems to slow down to a steadier tempo. It may be, however, that the drive and ambition common to early manhood in our societies has diverted attention from deeper problems of personality development which have been repressed, or set aside for the moment. With the slowing down of his outward drive which has centered around family, work, and social position, these unsolved earlier problems tend to revive and to present themselves as challenges to the later development of mature manhood. So the man in his forties faces the task of final integration, of the completion of his individuation process. This is a time of unrest for many men, of vague depressions, of dissatisfaction with their life-achievement, of a renewed questioning of their life-ideals, their personal philosophy, and their religious attitudes.

LONELINESS AND SPIRITUAL FATHERHOOD

The celibate priest is particularly vulnerable in facing this crisis of his manhood, especially if he has not fully found himself through the meeting of earlier challenges of growth. It is easy for the priest to be satisfied with a false identity, to be playing a part in life rather than being himself. He may be playing the part of the efficient administrative boss, of the withdrawn, self-effacing man of prayer, of the popular man-of-the-world, of the successful builder-financier—worst of all, he can be a petty tyrant playing the part of God. If there is this unreality and deep divisiveness in his self-identity, if he has never really found himself as a priest giving the whole of his real person in love, he may find that middle age will lead him only into further evasions, further flights from reality.

Even for the priest who has grown into late manhood realistically through the maturity of his active priesthood, middle age brings its further challenge of growth. His position, humanly speaking, is a lonely one as he looks around his parish and his circle of friends and relatives. He sees the men of his own age apparently settled securely with their wives and growing children; perhaps some of them are enjoying the happiness of grandchildren. If the early crisis in a priest's life centers round the loneliness of a man without a wife, the middle age crisis is often focussed on the emptiness of a man without a son or daughter. This basic loneliness and emptiness may be well below the surface of a priest's life. On the surface he may come to the shock of middle age and see that his life is more than half over—he may become sharply conscious of the waning and uncertain years ahead. He views his life-achievement, and sees little enough; he may honestly see that the reality is vastly different from the shining ideals of his early priesthood. He may look around and see that his friends are successful in business and professional fields, and wonder what he has to show for his life. He looks at other priests of his own age and sees that many of them seem to have gone ahead of him in scholastic achievement, in administration, in pastoral zeal, in the importance of the work given them—likely enough some of them are bishops.

This existential loneliness, this emptiness of spirit, this feeling of non-achievement, is strikingly pictured in many modern novels on the life of priests. Graham Greene has his priest in *The Power and the Glory* reflecting just before his execution:

What an impossible fellow I am, and how useless. I have done nothing for anybody. I might just as well have never lived . . . he felt only an immense disappointment because he had to go to God empty-handed, with nothing done at all.[5]

And Morris West puts similar thoughts of emptiness in the mind of his Father Meredith when he receives the news that his sickness is incurable:

[5] Graham Greene, *The Power and the Glory*, London: Heinemann, 1940, p. 273. Cf. American edition, New York: Viking, 1946.

There was the bitterness, the sour taste of failure and disillusion. What of merit could he tally and take with him to the judgment? What would he leave behind for which men would want to remember him? He had never fathered a child nor planted a tree, nor set one stone upon another for house or monument . . . He had done everything that was demanded of him, yet he would die empty and within a month his name would be a blown dust on the desert of the centuries.[6]

These priestly thoughts are not mere fancies of fiction. For every man who has grown into the maturity of his own identity feels the need, by middle age, to be leaving something behind him, to be passing on something of himself, to be seeing something of his own manhood beginning again in a new generation. A man has a need of fatherhood, as a woman must fulfill herself in being a mother. The priest ideally fulfills himself in this way, as Pius XII pointed out, in the passing on to other men and women of the new life of the risen Christ. But it is only where the dynamism of faith is very strong and vigorous that this concept, however beautiful, is able to provide the priest, at the emotional level, with a sense of fulfillment in middle life.

This spiritual fatherhood is brought nearer to the priest when he has an active part in the formation of a young priest; it is to be hoped that the new schemes of active formation for young students will provide amply for this master-disciple relationship, which is capable of infusing new meaning and hope into the life of a middle-aged priest. This point is stressed by Daniel Pezeril in his novel, *Rue Notre Dame*; he has his old canon saying to the cardinal:

It's a disaster that your parishes and your clergy are not organized on the lines of a priestly college, and that they are not entrusted

[6] Morris West, *The Devil's Advocate*, London: Heinemann, 1959, p. 5. Cf. American edition, New York: Morrow, 1959.

with one or two aspirants to Orders. Once a community has accepted these boys . . . every priest in it would find his stature increased . . . Give your seminarists a place in what is really their first family, not only for their own benefit, but still more for ours, so that we may not come to die without ever knowing fatherhood.[7]

This intimate fatherhood of the priest helps him establish within himself a fruitful sense of self-identity as he sees something of himself take new shape and promise in the life of a young disciple.

Erikson found elements of this crisis of middle age in the life of Luther; speaking of his breakdown at this time, he comments:

The crisis of generativity occurs when a man looks at what he has generated, or helped to generate, and finds it good or wanting, when his life work as part of the productivity of his time gives him some sense of being on the side of a few angels or makes him feel stagnant. All this in turn, offers him either promise of an old age that can be faced with a sense of integrity, and in which he can say, 'All in all, I would do this over again,' or confronts him with a sense of waste, of despair.[8]

We have seen how each of these crises of growth, in late adolescence, in early manhood, and in middle age, present the man who is a celibate priest with a challenge to grow. His growth must be equally, and at the same time, psychological and spiritual. He must find in his celibacy the dynamic elements of mature manly development, so that he is becoming more and more fulfilled in his manhood; his celibacy at the same time is a spiritual focus of love in the Spirit, in which he finds an ever-deepening energy of love for Jesus and his people. We have emphasized that this is psychologically possible and meaningful; at the same time it flows from

[7] Daniel Pezeril, *Rue Notre Dame,* London: Burns & Oates, 1953, p. 24.
[8] Erik H. Erikson, *Young Man Luther,* pp. 236–237.

the concept of dedicated apostleship seen fully in the person of Jesus, in his death as the suffering servant and in his rising to new life. So are we led back to the theological conclusion that finds the final meaning of the priest's celibacy at the eschatological level.

It is in the priest's attitude to his own death that he must find a pattern of meaning for the later part of his life. The eschatological dimension of his own celibacy-dedication must have meaning for himself if it is to have a message for other men. Psychology, in its present form still an infant discipline, has even less to say to us about death than it has about mature middle age. Carl Jung, as much a philosopher as a psychiatrist, has much to say about the social roles of old age, and does not hesitate to discuss the difficulty many modern people have in accepting the thought of a new life after death, since science has nothing to say on this issue, one way or another. But he concludes:

I have observed that a directed life is in general better, richer, and healthier than an aimless one, and that it is better to go forwards with the stream of time than backwards against it. To the psychotherapist, an old man who cannot bid farewell to life appears as feeble and sickly as a young man who is unable to embrace it. And as a matter of fact, in many cases it is a question of the self-same childish covetousness, of the same fear, the same obstinacy and willfulness, in the one as in the other. As a physician I am convinced that it is hygienic—if I may use the word—to discover in death a goal towards which one can strive; and that shrinking away from it is something unhealthy and abnormal which robs the second half of life of its purpose.[9]

Erikson, too, leads up to the point of death. He outlines three stages of development in adulthood—intimacy and

[9] Carl G. Jung, *Modern Man in Search of a Soul,* London: Routledge and Kegan Paul, 1933, pp. 128–129. Cf. American edition, New York: Harcourt.

distantiation, generativity, and integrity, each with their negative counterpart. Speaking of the despair and disgust which is the failure to achieve the goal of final integrity, he says:

> I can add, clinically, that the lack or loss of this accrued ego integration is signified by despair and an often unconscious fear of death: the one and only life cycle is not accepted as the ultimate of life. Despair expresses the feeling that the time is short, too short for the attempt to start another life and to try out alternate roads to integrity. Such a despair is often hidden behind a show of disgust, a misanthropy, or a chronic contemptuous displeasure with particular institutions and particular people—a disgust and displeasure which (where not allied with constructive ideas and a life of cooperation), only signify the individual's contempt of himself.[10]

The priest's celibacy is a public testimony to the values which he perceives beyond the highest values of love in this present life; the only psychological justification for his free renunciation of marriage is that he has a deep personal conviction of an even higher value of love which extends beyond the point where the psychologist stops. The priest's celibacy has an eschatological dimension of meaning; the priest by the sign of his life testifies that the world is advancing towards the final time of the Lord's coming, that we are a people waiting for the Lord. This social significance must have its counterpart at the personal level also. The priest, in the inner meaning of his own life, must be true to his celibacy. He must, particularly in his later years, achieve the final wholehearted integration spoken of by the psychologists. He must be able to link together in a final synthesis all the human values of his growth and self-identity into a pattern of worthwhile meaning for himself and for others. This synthesis must lead him to that confidence in his destiny, that trusting assurance of the permanence of love, which will

[10] Erik H. Erikson, *Identity and the Life Cycle*, New York: International Universities Press, 1959, p. 98.

enable him to feel that death is the final act of his human maturity as well as his ultimate self-donation to the love of the Holy Spirit.

It is in this attitude of total surrender to the reality of death that he achieves the final meaning of his celibacy-dedication. We have seen that every act of love involves self-possession, self-donation, and a full recognition of the personal reality of the other. The priest, coming in the later years of his life to the full possession of himself in mature integrity, is growing towards the full capacity of his existential freedom—he is able at last to give himself totally into the welcoming arms of the love which is waiting for him. In this final surrender of his being to love, he joins the company of the *anawim,* those who recognize in self-surrender the ultimate reality of God and enter into the full possession of the promised Kingdom. De Chardin, with his capacity for seeing a fourth dimension of creative love shining through all that is ordinary, speaks of death as "That leap out of ourselves which must in the end deliver us from the bondage of ourselves into the service of the divine sovereignty."[11]

In this attitude to death, the priest is modeling himself on the death of Jesus, who, on the cross, surrendered himself totally into the hands of his Father. It is this final act of self-donation in love which wins for the priest the promised fulfillment of his celibacy. For when Peter asked Jesus: "What of us? We have forsaken all that was ours and followed thee," Jesus answered, "I promise you, everyone who has forsaken home, or parents, or brethren, or wife, or children for the sake of the kingdom of God, will receive, in this present world, many times their worth, and in the world to come, everlasting life." (Luke 18. 28–30). The celibacy of the priest is a public witness to this promise of life without

[11] Pierre Teilhard de Chardin, *The Divine Milieu,* New York: Harper, 1960, p. 88.

end, and to the fact that the life beyond death is an entering into love, that it is the final fulfillment of the whole love-energy of the human person. This is the meaning of the unusual dedication of a priest's life; it is the meaning which he must be achieving in his maturity as he grows into his full self-identity. The achievement of this final meaning for his life is the crisis-task of his later years and should be the serene possession of his old age.

In showing this whole development of a priest's life, from later adolescence to old age, we have emphasized the difficulties and crises on the way to the fulfillment of the high meaning of his celibacy. We have seen that each of these crisis periods is a challenge to his further psychological and spiritual growth. It should now be more evident why many psychologists regard celibacy as a commitment of full maturity rather than of early manhood. That the difficulties we have mentioned are not to be taken lightly is emphasized by the psychologist Ignace Lepp in his discussion of the chastity-dedication:

The depth psychologist hesitates to endorse unreservedly the radical renunciation of celibacy by anyone who is not in the category of the great mystics. I know from experience how serious the danger of neurotic distortion is in the case of those who are not genuinely called to the mystical life, or of those who fail to do all in their power to meaure up to the harsh demands which such a vocation can make upon them. Such persons usually are astonished by the strength of their erotic impulses. The bizarre behavior of a great many 'old bachelors' and 'old maids'—and there are a number of priests and sisters among them—is not unrelated to the fact of their chastity, a chastity that is not counterbalanced by a genuinely mystical life. As Pascal wrote, 'He who would play the angel, ends by playing the beast.' There is no question of condemning chastity in the name of psychological health. It is simply a matter of pointing out, on the basis of experience, the fact that in normally constituted human beings the libido cannot be channeled in a different direction without injury to sexuality unless it finds itself entirely consumed in the service of higher psychic activity. No one should entertain any illusion about the facility with which such mystical sublimation can be effected.[12]

In my later years at the seminary, before ordination, we received occasional lectures on the priestly life from a middle-aged priest who used to assure us, with great solemnity, that we would never be better priests than on the day of our ordination; all our striving, our improvement, should take place before ordination, because it was not likely to go on afterwards. I am happy to remember that I rejected this instinctively as utter nonsense; and at this point I feel that it is necessary to emphasize most firmly that a priest can and should be constantly growing in his priesthood as in his manhood. It has been necessary to stress the situational conflicts in the life of the modern priest, and we shall see something more of them in the next chapter. However, these conflicts, even when added to the burden of personal anxiety and instability which we all carry to some extent, should present themselves to each priest as a stimulus towards further psychological and spiritual growth. Any priest who feels that there has been no such growth since his ordination would be well advised to seek expert help and counseling.

We should regard it as a common task of the priesthood to re-examine its outward structure to meet the needs of each succeeding age and the men of that age. This will involve us in a critical examination of training schemes, forms of life-commitment, of life-style, of modalities of the spiritual life of the priest. Our psychology, our sociology, our spirituality should be subject to constant renewal and re-energizing. But at the same time, those who, like myself, are priests of the present day, must accept and surrender themselves to the reality of the Church of today. We embrace our life as it is,

[12] Ignace Lepp, *The Psychology of Loving*, Baltimore: Helicon, 1964, p. 211.

even when, in some cases, we might feel that it does not suit us very well in some ways. Accepting ourselves as we are, our life as priests with its present social, legal, and spiritual form, our neighbors in the priesthood and the laity as they are, is a very necessary step in our own growth towards maturity as men and as priests. It is a step, and not an easy one, which must be taken before we begin to discuss the suggestions I have made for the reform and renewal of the life of the secular priests of the West. Without this wholehearted and joyful acceptance of what is, we are in danger of withdrawing from reality into the land of dreams, and our proposals for renewal might seem more like the whining of children or the daydreams of adolescents than the sensible discussion of mature men.

10:

THE TEMPTATION OF POWER

I SPENT an evening recently with a psychologist friend who has had wide experience in dealing with priests. We were talking about the making of this book, and especially about freedom. The priest, my friend suggested, should be the most free among men. Ontologically, the priest's celibacy-dedication related him immediately to the center of reality in total devotion; the priest's dedication to God, his service of the community, and his keen sense of the permanent values of love, is itself a liberation from all those restricting and particular limitations which the family man must suffer in the focusing of his life around the love and service of his family.

"But psychologically," he pointed out, "with many priests this does not happen; they carry their celibacy as a burden rather than a liberation, as a shroud rather than a victory; there is no sign in them of the truth that makes them free. So their celibacy is no longer a witness to men of the joyful abandon of total love, it no longer testifies to the victory of the Resurrection. These priests seem to be unable to accept their freedom—this, after all, is why they have chosen celibacy, in order to be free for love, to be free instruments of the Holy Spirit. This is the problem of your book, Father, that you have priests who are theoretically dedicated to these liberating ideals, but who are actually unfree in their psychological development. Thus, you have your man of inner contradiction. And I think that while what you have written, along Freudian lines, about the frustration and non-fulfillment of the whole sexual urge in the priest, is very true, we must also look at the priest's conscious decisions, at the deliberate direction which he gives to his life. And here we can get more light from Adler than from Freud; this is as much a problem of the will to power as it is a sexual problem."

"You can think of many mature priests," he continued, "who are not notably handicapped by any neurotic limitations in their personality, who simply seem to have chosen a wrong direction, made a wrong use of the freedom which celibacy gives them. Instead of being free and open in their love, they become closed-up and self-contained, men of authority rather than men of love. And I think that this is in some way due to the training they have received. The central values they saw in the seminary were those of authority and obedience; when they come to be curates, they are subject to the firm authority of parish priest and bishop, and the important thing in their lives is still obedience to authority. Inevitably, they look forward to the day when they themselves will be in authority; even as curates, they tend to think of the priesthood in these terms—in the beginning, their extreme youthfulness, and lack of leadership ability makes them ill at ease in dealing with mature people, and they tend to retreat back to the authority of their priesthood. So gradually the priest becomes an instrument of authority, closed to the reality of the persons around him, rather than an instrument of the Spirit freely recognizing in love the freedom and reality of each person he meets. I think this is a very important factor in the formation of the closed-up, slightly bitter, authoritarian type of middle-aged priest you have described."

Our talking on these lines lasted some hours. We discussed

the kind of inner conflict that builds up in the authoritative type of priest. He is reading in his Bible that he must be an instrument of love, and this may be the burden of much of his preaching and his reading, of much of his conscious idealism; then slowly it begins to dawn on him that he is not a man of personal love at all, but a capable administrator, a good organizer, a shrewd financier, a functionary. He can be so committed to this false self-image that he feels it too late to change. The administrative type of priest is like the father of a family who has controlled his children with firm authority and little personal love; this may seem to work well when the children are young, but when they come to the oppositional stage of adolescence and rebel against authority, the father finds that he has no other way of approaching them, that he cannot talk to them as persons. So too, the priest may come gradually to the realization that he has really nothing to give, that he is empty of love, that his life has no meaning for him.

The young priest may easily make this wrong decision as to what he is, as to what he is going to project of himself into his parish family. He may be tempted to put always in the first place order rather than love. A parish, in our Western societies, has little natural order—it is a house here, an apartment there, a haphazard collection of families and individuals without any other community bond than common faith, and the priest can easily view his greatest task as the formation of an orderly parish community under the authority of the priest-father. The Church in Europe in the early Middle Ages saw its task this way, and gradually took on a number of authoritarian and legal forms which we are now revising. Adler showed us that the power impulse is strong in the individual as well as in groups and communities. So we have the whole present human style of the Church as well as the apparent needs of the parish to be an ordered community, reinforcing in the priest what is a strong natural urge of his nature. While the need of order in the Church and in the parish is meant to be a challenge to us to find the synthesis of order and freedom in love, it very often serves only as a spur and excuse for the exercise of power, for the repression of individuality in others, for treating them as objects rather than persons.

For the priest caught in this web of instinct and circumstance, his aim very easily becomes the rewards of power. He will be seeking more power, more responsibility, more authority. He will see that those priests who are successful and firm administrators, who keep good order in their parishes and a firm hand on their curates, are the ones who are rewarded with the bigger parishes, the responsible diocesan positions, the bishoprics. While this is not always objectively true, there is quite enough truth in it, in most places, for this to seem the real thing for a priest whose whole mind and life-aim is moving in this direction.

Let us look at the kind of influence these pressures have on the development of the young priest. He has been, most likely, brought up in a family atmosphere of love, and his initial decision to go to a seminary is based on the ideal of service of the Lord and the people in terms of love, with maybe only a little mixed motivation to cloud it. Because he is a young man of our society, he has probably a strong urge to do well, to be a success in life, to do better than others, to climb the ladder of social approval. In terms of the priesthood, he will be idealizing some priest he knows, whom he feels has been a great success in the Church. In the seminary, while there will be a great emphasis on the idealism of Christian love and service, there will probably be, too, the hard practical lessons of authority, obedience, and of the success of those students who respond smoothly to the authority system of the seminary. While his idealism will remain, it may well become divorced from the immediate realities of his life, and develop into a kind of private enthusiasm taking second place to his need to develop into an obedient, dutiful, prudent, careful young man who will do well in the ministry and be well thought of by his superiors.

About the age of twenty-four, he will be a young priest, and will be assigned as curate to a parish priest who is middle-aged or elderly. The presence of the bright young curate is always something of a personal challenge to the older priest; it may also be felt as a potential challenge to his authority and position in the parish. Here is a young man just out of school, with spiritual powers of priesthood equal to those of this parish priest. He is up-to-date in his studies and in his understanding of the new ways in the Church. It is understandable if the parish priest has the uneasy suspicion that anything he can do, his curate might do better; quite possibly, the curate is himself fairly sure of this.

It is inevitable that the parish priest will tend to retreat to his authority, and to feel that he must train his curate in terms of duty, order, and obedience. It is in these areas that the parish priest feels that he has an official as well as a natural superiority. This may, in fact, be an old man's only self-defense against the intrusion of youthful enthusiasm into the settled order which he has created around himself. This is one of the many reasons why the young student should be introduced to parish work as a catechist and as a deacon, rather than as a fully-ordained priest.

If the young priest responds well to this kind of training in order and authority, it will often be at the expense of much of his idealism. If he responds with resentment, his loss will be greater. In either case, it is likely that he will be reinforcing in himself the urge to power rather than the urge to love. The parish priest, too, is the loser in this type of relationship, since he is losing a special opportunity of being a father. We have seen that every man must find the full flowering of his manliness in fatherhood, as every woman must find some kind of motherhood. Unfortunately, while the parish priest might think in terms of being a father rather than merely a superior to his young and inexperienced curate, the loving qualities of this relationship will be inhibited not only by the whole power-style of his life and that of the curate, but even more by the cultural concept of a fatherhood in Western societies. In our society, it is the man who exercises authority, at least in popular thinking; fatherhood is popularly felt as a function of authority more than of love. Our ideal father is the strong-willed dominant person who provides well for his family and wields a firm authority over his children. Man as a husband is expected to be a loving person; as a father he is expected to love his children in a rather abstract way, but not so much to be loving towards them once they grow beyond early childhood. The father who does not have strong authority over his growing children is considered to be weak, to be unmanly. Instead of creating the ideal synthesis of love and order, the father in our society tends toward an imbalance of order and authority. This is the picture of fatherhood which the priest inherits from his culture; it colors equally his effort to be the father of his people and the attempt he makes to be fatherly towards the young curate.

We have seen, therefore, a three-fold pressure on the priest which leads him towards this imbalance in the relationship of authority and love in his practical living. In the first place, because of a personal celibacy which is very often not integrated into his life-style, he tends to seek compensation in power. Whether we view this from the viewpoint of one school of psychology or another, all psychologists point to the tendency of our nature to compensate in some way. Whenever the satisfaction of one urgency of our being is blocked, if this very blocking is not free, deliberated, and well-integrated, there will be a tendency, conscious and unconscious, to find strong substitute satisfaction in some other direction. We might also analyze the frustrated priest's love of possessions and external grandeur, or his love of pleasure and comfort, in these terms. We have discussed rather the urge for power because this is not so obvious to the priest, because it is more subject to conscious rationalization and to unconscious dynamisms, and because the whole power structure of the Church, from the Pope down to the curate, is at present under discussion. It is important that this discussion, at all levels, should take note of the psychological and sociological dynamisms involved in the exercise of power. Because the priest is a man of himself, of his society, and of the present-day Church, he is inevitably subject to these personal and social pressures.

The second pressure in the use of power is educational. The structure and atmosphere of the seminary is very easily interpreted by the young mind of the late adolescent in terms of authority and obedience, with all other values, in practice, being subsidiary. This institutional pressure is continued when the young man emerges as a priest; the same values seem to be dominant. If he is to do well as a priest, if he is to get on and be a success in life, he easily feels that the way of careful submission to authority, and the firm "manly" exercise of his own authority as a priest, will lead him to the desirable roles of parish priest, monsignor, and bishop.

The third aspect of this pressure is cultural. The father-image of our society seems to reinforce the pressures which are coming from within the personality of the priest, and from the teaching he seems to receive from the seminary, from his parish priest, and from his bishop. The priest who vows himself in celibacy, feels instinctively, if not also consciously, that because he is not to be a husband and a father, he must fulfill his manhood and his fatherhood in some way or other. If he does not search out for himself the way of true celibacy which we have outlined in this book, he is very likely to be led by the social image of fatherhood in his

society, into the kind of attempted fulfillment of his manhood through power, that we have described. The priesthood
has the built-in avenues for this false priestly identity to
develop with a certain measure of self-satisfaction and social
prestige.

It was this whole tendency towards power that we see in
the Gospel story of the formation of the apostles. St. Luke
tells, in his account of the Last Supper, of the rivalry among
the apostles as to who was to be greatest in the kingdom.
Jesus told them,

> The kings of the gentiles lord it over them, and those who bear
> rule over them win the name of benefactors. With you it is not to
> be so; no difference is to be made, among you, between the greatest
> and the youngest of all, between him who commands and him who
> serves. Tell me, which is greater, the man who sits at table, or the
> man who serves him? Surely the man who sits at table; yet here am
> I among you as your servant (c. 22. vv. 25–27).

St. John tells the story of how, at the Supper, Jesus washed
the feet of the apostles, and told them that they must follow
his example, and wash the feet of one another. "No slave,"
he told them, "can be greater than his master, no apostle
greater than he by whom he was sent" (c. 13. v. 16).

If the priest is to find the true meaning of his celibacy for
himself, and give witness of this to men, he must not only
speak with the authority of his Lord, but also live in his love
by being the devoted servant of his people. Men must find
in him not only the teaching of Christ, but the meaning of
this teaching for their personal lives. They will see this personal vision of the way of Jesus not only in the Gospel but
also in the way the priest lives, the way he reflects in his life
the total dedication of Christian love, the totally free aban-
donment of himself in love not only to the Father, but also
to his people in his role of humble and willing servant.

II:

THE FULL MEANING OF A PRIEST'S CELIBACY

WE MUST NOW MAKE AN ATTEMPT to bring together into a final focus of meaning all the rays of light we have gathered from psychology and theology, so as to make a coherent picture of the celibacy of the priest. Much of the reasoning of this book has been from a negative approach. From looking critically at the celibacy of the priesthood during history, and at the celibacy of the priests of today with its many negative tendencies, we have seen what this priestly commitment should not be. This chapter aims to gather together the positive ideals we have gained from all this and to integrate it with what we have learned from a direct reference to the sources, both theological and psychological.

The theologian, Edward Schillebeeckx, developed a three-fold dimension of meaning for the priest's celibacy, a Christological dimension, an ecclesiological dimension, and an eschatological dimension. Through his celibacy the priest is related directly to Christ, to the Church, and to the ultimate, final reality. In terms of the psychology of human growth, this triple dimension corresponds to the development of the manhood-maturity of the priest in terms of his self-identity as a priest, of his relatedness to other persons, and of his final integrity.

The priest's personal relationship to Christ is obviously

of central meaning for his life; we would expect, then, to find a central meaning for his life-commitment of celibacy in this relationship. It cannot be too often emphasized, in view of the number of people who consider it rather unpleasant that sex tends to creep so much into religion and psychology, that celibacy is a sexual dedication in a priest. It is a personal consecration of his sexual function, and in particular of its normal fulfillment in marriage; he consecrates this function to a religious ideal in terms of the love of the Spirit of Jesus which transcends the high values of marriage and, indeed, all the love-values of this world of men. The priest's dedication is a witnessing to these supernatural values revealed to us in the person and message of Jesus. In the whole consecration of his life he is, in a sense, carrying on the person and message of his Lord whose priesthood he shares.

From considering the meaning of the sexual function in a man, both in terms of its fulfillment in marriage and in terms of its influence on the whole growth of his being into mature manhood, we saw that the fulfillment of this function is in the stable interpersonal relationship of love, marked by the quality of complete devotion to the personal reality of the other. We saw that this must lead to self-donation, self-surrender, in which the man finds his own final meaning and identity in the welfare and joy of the other. The celibate priest achieves his growth into manhood and forms his mature self-identity as a priest through his personal relationship with Jesus. He offers the utter devotion of his whole person in self-surrender to his Lord, in response to the intimate personal love for him which he sees in Jesus, and the total surrender of death for him which he sees in the redeeming act of Christ. This is a relationship which is over and above both the sexual and the other stable inter-human personal relationships; it is capable of fulfilling and transcending their values.

This interpersonal relationship of love and devotion leads, on the priest's part, to an identification of himself with Christ. He sees himself, as a priest, being "another Christ." In the Church's liturgy, and in the active charity of his service to men, he acts in the name of Jesus, surrendering himself to the reality of the Christ-functions he carries out. However, as he grows towards his final maturity as man and priest, he must go a stage further from identification to full self-identity. Carl Jung posed the difficulty of this final step into maturity:

Are we to understand the 'imitation of Christ' in the sense that we are to live our own proper lives as truly as he lived his in all its implications? It is no easy matter to live a life that is modeled on Christ's, but it is unspeakably harder to live one's own life as truly as Christ lived his.[1]

Whatever psychological term we use, whether we speak of the self-image, the self-concept, the self-system, the ego ideal, the ego identity, we recognize that the man of full maturity faces the task of integrating all the various identifications and self-ideals of childhood and early manhood into one final picture, which I have called his self-identity. This picture shows the full meaning of his whole life and self, both to himself and to others. It is not enough for the priest to be a man imitating Christ; he must do the work of Christ, carry his message, show his genuineness, and the relevance of his love, not by being an imitation of someone, but by being fully and maturely himself.

St. John the Baptist faced this problem of his self-identity when the Jewish authorities came to ask him who he was. He answered with a clear "No" when they asked him if he were the Messiah, or the promised prophet, or Elias come back to life. When they pressed him, he told them simply

---

[1] Carl G. Jung, *op. cit.*, p. 273.

that he was the voice from the desert foretold by Isaias, with a message to the people to prepare the way for the Lord. He saw his own life reach its full meaning the next day when he pointed out the Lamb of God, and concluded "Now I have seen him, and have borne my witness that this is the Son of God." (John c. 1. vv. 19–34.) St. Gregory comments very simply on this incident in St. John's life: "Though his virtue was so eminent that he could have been taken for the Christ, he chose to remain solidly himself. He did not lose his self-possession to the empty vanity of human opinion."[2]

The priest, also, must be solidly himself, and must not let anything lead him into a false identity; he must come, by the loving response of faith, into his own authentic existence. He will see his life gradually find its full meaning through his growth in interpersonal love with Jesus, and through his deeper understanding of the kind of witness which he will make to men through the whole dedication of his life in celibacy. It is only in this full self-possession that he is able to make his full self-donation in love. For he must give away not only the false self-images which have tended to lead him away from himself, but also, finally, he makes his authentic self-surrender to the ultimate reality of love.

The priest's dedication of celibacy has, further, a community dimension of meaning. This may be called ecclesiological, for it is in the priest's relationship to the ecclesia, the gathering together of God's people in Christ, that he discovers a further wealth of meaning in his celibacy. His celibacy, as we have seen, is a challenge to him to make himself free for love and service. The priest learns to see his function as a leader of the Christian community in terms of the distinctive teaching of Jesus on authority as a service of love; so his celibacy becomes a witness to the loving-service

---

[2] Quoted in *The Divine Office*, Vol. I, Collegeville, Minn.: The Liturgical Press, 1963, p. 1099.

of the Savior. Because his life-commitment is to the total service of the people, he finds in the life and person of Jesus the high qualities of love for all those in need; he sees patience and tenderness and compassionate kindness, and an utter devotion which leads to the final love of the redemption.

In this spending of himself in the service of Lord and people, the priest is witnessing to love through the total commitment of his celibacy. He is also finding for himself a growing maturity of loving, which leads him to the fulfillment of the deep urge to love which gives meaning to his sexual function. In the total service of Christ's people he can find the full development of his manhood. In his warmhearted acceptance of the reality of others, he will be led to the rich qualities of loving tenderness, compassion, and sympathy which he sees in the person of Jesus. This becomes for him a way of holiness as well as a way of self-growth into full maturity. He faces within himself the dichotomy of being a man who loves no one but his Lord, and at the same time being a man who loves all men, all that is human, all that is good. Each priest's synthesis of these opposites is something personal to himself, but it is always based on the extra dimension of this world's reality. Like a fourth dimension, the priest sees, beyond the ordinary lives and affairs of men, the divine reality of creative love. He is able fully to share the lives of his fellows, to play his part as a man, to be as keenly dedicated to the progress of men as he is a compassionate sharer of their suffering, their hunger, their anxiety, their need for love.

It is because the priest is aware of the love behind reality that he suffers with his Lord in the sins of men. For he sees sin as the retreat from reality, the running away from love, the fear of man when he is afraid to be free. He knows from the Scripture that the original sin was the lie of men trying to be what they were not, the false image of self set against reality, the retreat from the outward reality of loving, into the slavery of being turned inward on the self. The priest is interested in this intensely, for he has the message of the good news of the way of return to love. He has the Spirit of Jesus, the divine Love, within him as the energizing center of his life. He is able, with Jesus, to make his own the message of liberating love in Isaias: "The Spirit of the Lord is upon me; he has anointed me, and sent me out to preach the gospel to the poor, to restore the brokenhearted; to bid the prisoners go free, and the blind have sight; to set the oppressed at liberty." (Luke c. 4. vv. 18, 19.)

The celibacy of the priest has its ultimate dimension of meaning in the *eschaton,* the final end of our reality. This eschatological view, as we have seen, generally becomes a living force in the priest in late maturity, when he is faced with the task of achieving his full integrity, his final life-view. In his direct personal relationship with Jesus, the priest is led to the image of his Savior offering himself on the cross; he finds in this element of the Gospel the key to his own full identity as a priest. In his loving-service of the people of God, the priest sees the qualities he requires in the image of Jesus walking among men. And in finding for his own life the eschatological dimension of his celibacy, the priest must look to the Resurrection of Jesus and to the mystery of his second coming.

We have seen that the celibacy dedication is a witnessing to the reality of life after death. The celibate priest is the living sign of the waiting people, the community waiting for the final fulfillment in the coming of the Lord. The priest is witnessing that this finality, just as the finality of the lives of each of us, is not so much an ending, but a new beginning of love. The priest, by foregoing so much of this life's expression of love, is a living sign of a further love, a testimony that love will never end. All men honor the testimony of blood; they recognize in the martyr a messenger who commands us to listen by the wholeheartedness of his conviction.

The priest gives in his life this testimony of death for his conviction. For in him the human race dies by his deliberate decision to forego wife and family; because he passes on life to no one of his own, he earns the right to witness to the love that reaches beyond death, beyond all the reality of this world.

To make this dimension of his celibacy a living meaning in his own life, the priest must not only be mature enough to be achieving his own integral life-view out of all the contributing and conflicting forces that have gone to make him, but he must also be coming to the spiritual maturity of faith. For this meaning of a human life is a leap into the dark; it is more than learning, it is a dark venture into the final abandon of loving. St. Paul meant something of this when he told us that we must believe with our hearts, for this kind of trusting faith must come out of love. (Romans c. 10. v. 10.) So this meaning, as every other meaning we have found for the celibacy of the priest, is centered in love.

The priest will find this love in the Paschal mystery of Christ, in the Savior who passes from death to life. The Spirit of Jesus, living and energizing in the central being of the priest, is himself the way by which the priest finds in his celibacy a passing from death to life; it is this Spirit, the love-in-person of the Trinity, who gives to the dedicated life of the priest its final stamp of meaning. For the Spirit of creative Love is the origin of all reality, and it is he who will be the final fulfillment of all things in love when the cycle of time is complete.

Every Christian is a witness, each in his own way, of the reality of the Holy Spirit of Love. What the priest witnesses through his celibacy, the father of a family, or the mother, must witness in a different framework of life, with different tensions and problems. Because the priest's witness is a more direct one, the greater is the tragedy when it does not ring true, when it is obscured by elements that are false to the true message of love. It is for this reason that we have given so much attention in this book to all those factors and influences, in the personal growth of the priest, in his training, in his way of living in the Church and as a member of his wider society, which tend to distort the meaning of his life. The present time of renewal within the Church may be a suitable time for the kind of rethinking of the priest's life which must be the prelude to the renewal of priestly celibacy as a living witness of the meaning of love.

12:

THE PRIEST IN CHANGING TIMES

THAT THE WESTERN PRIEST OF TODAY must adapt to a rapidly changing society is without question. The Church as a whole is going through a period of inner renewal in order to meet the challenge of this change. A great deal has already been said and written about the new role that nuns might play in this renewed Church. The need is equally evident of a re-thinking of the priest's life and work. The whole question of the form of dedication suitable for the priest of the future needs to be examined in this light.

Many modern writers have seen man's history as a steady, if erratic, growth towards personalism. They describe how, in primitive animist societies, man is tightly bound in a cosmic unity of nature and supernature. He is only vaguely aware of himself as an individual person, and this means little to him in comparison with his unity in his society and with the rest of nature—stars, sun, moon, winds, forest, earth, crops, and animals. Then there is a stage of development, represented in European history by the Middle Ages, when man has still his firm social unity, but has largely lost his feeling of solidarity with the rest of nature. Already he is begin-ning to see himself over against nature, as its master. His social order is relatively static, and the individual is largely conscious of himself as a member of a certain class or group within society. This place is normally fixed for him, and is regarded as the will of God. Both geographical and social mobility are very limited. With the later Middle Ages and the time of the Renaissance, we already see the beginnings of the breakup of this static social structure and the steady growth of man's self-consciousness as an individual person, which has gone on steadily through our own day. The present emphasis within our society on individual, personal human values, and on the importance of personal growth and maturity, is seen as part of man's long struggle towards self-consciousness and fulfillment, in a new kind of free-relating community. It is this framework of orientation which has produced the individual, analytical, and the developmental psychology of our time, with its social overtones stressing the I-Thou, the interpersonal.

The Christian Church, which began its growth with a strong emphasis on individual freedom and fulfillment in reaction against the empire-ideal, went through a gradual adaptation and assimilation to it as the Christian community in Europe became dominant and built itself into the medieval society; we see the Church, as part of this society, taking on a monarchical, feudal, and legal social form. It is this set of human forms which are under reconsideration today, as the Church is meditating on the kind of adaptation needed to show herself as the community of God's people in a highly individual, personalist world of men which sees the community as a dynamic interaction of free persons.

The priest within the Church has gone through a similar phase of development. The social form of the priesthood has always corresponded in large extent to the human ideal of the age. In the early Church we see in the clergy the non-conformist, highly personal character, as the Church, and much of society, reacted against the old empire-ideal. In the early Middle Ages, the time during which celibacy was gradually imposed as low, we see the priest slowly emerging as the feudal servant of the Lord, bound in total allegiance to his God-willed position and function, the custodian without heirs of the Church's patrimony. He is, like most of his fellows, an outer-directed man in a traditional society, a man bound by law and allegiance.

In the world of today the priest wants to be a man of today, to share in the whole personalist development and growth of modern man, to baptize all that is truly good and human in this movement. Yet, apart from a modest improvement in his general education and social position, he is still largely bound by the social forms of the Middle Ages. His personal striving for inner-directed maturity and fulfillment is in conflict, as yet in vague and indetermined ways, with the feudal allegiance and law-bound submissiveness of his medieval predecessors. As the aloneness and insecurity of modern men often lead them into temporary submission to totalitarian societies, some modern secular priests feel that the solution to their difficulties lies in being bound more firmly in religious community life and seminary-like regulation, in which they will find security in conforming to a large group. Others feel that the priest, like modern man as a whole, must think out his own personal implications of creative love and service out in the midst of the free society of dedicated and mature men.

The gradual change in the human ideal in Western society is seen clearly in the history of education. The aim and purpose of the education of young men within the feudal society of the early middle ages was very different from that of the school of today; this is so not only in the obvious terms of the curriculum, but in the kind of personal development aimed at in the school. In a recent essay by a namesake of mine, the evolution of the ideal of a gentleman, as seen in education, is traced from medieval to modern times: "The tracing from the old ideal to the new," this writer states, "can be seen as a trend from the group image of medieval society to the individual image of today's flexible, socially mobile society." He concludes that this ideal

has probably changed more in the last century than during the five centuries preceding it. Yet at the same time, the change in the ideal has been a continuance of the trend which has been evident since the breakdown of the feudal system. This trend, as mentioned earlier, has been away from the group image of man to the individual image . . . The social order was static and each person was tied to the role and status into which he had been born. The commercial revolution, the renaissance, the reformation, the enlightenment, the French Revolution, the industrial revolution, and the technological revolution were just so many aspects of the trend for man to regard himself as an individual and not as a group . . . The ideal of a gentleman today seems to be that of the mature, socialized individual, with a fully developed personality . . . able to adapt and socialize himself to his own chosen position in society.[1]

The psychological importance of this evolution of the human ideal, particularly in our understanding of the modern marriage relationship, is stressed by Ignace Lepp in his *Psychology of Loving*. He points out that this transformation in the consciousness of Western man has been by imperceptible stages; from being a member of a collectivity, he has gradually become more and more of an autonomous individual. He comments:

It is not one of the psychologist's tasks to pass judgment on the value of the profound modification that has occurred in the consciousness of Western man. It is his task, however, to take note of it, and to draw from it the consequences he sees it to have for concrete behavior. But there seems to be no reason why the moralist or the sociologist—though both their disciplines possess a normative character—ought to interpret the psychological revolution which

[1] David P. O'Neill, "The Gentleman: The Evolution of an Ideal from Medieval to Modern Times," Unpublished essay.

has occurred as a catastrophe. It is true that the individualism which has taken the place of a collective consciousness carries with it certain serious dangers. But there are many signs today that already presage the emergence of a new form of consciousness, which can be called a communal consciousness. This new form of consciousness stresses equally the individual and interpersonal communion.[2]

We must all recognize in ourselves a twofold resistance to change. We find it difficult, especially in the later years of life, to realize that change has taken place at any deep level of life; while we notice, often with real anxiety, that the ways of people have changed since we were young, it is hard for us to admit that this could be due to deep changes in psychological and social structures—we are much more likely to put it down to the perversities of "the young people of today." Our second resistance is against the suggestion that these changes in people and in society could be changes for the better. It is as if we had a vested interest in the ways of our youth, in the values of our upbringing and education, in the society which we helped to make. When young people joyfully crusade against these ways and values, and assure us that the bad old days are gone, we tend to take a defensive attitude. While it is part of the function of older people to preserve ancient values, we must not let this function blind us to the fact that deep changes of the kind we have described are taking place in the individuals and societies of the West, and that it is these changes which are being reflected in the Church's present renewal. Priests, whether they admit it or not, whether they like it or not, are themselves part of this process of change.

Consequent on this evolutionary change in the human ideal, the importance of inherited social class is steadily lessening. The fixed role-functions within society, those of the

[2] Ignace Lepp, *op. cit.*, pp. 137–138.

medical man, the priest, the lawmaker, no longer command the automatic social status of former days. The priest of today is no longer given a universal respect as the educated man, the wise counselor, the leader in community affairs; in these functions he is largely superseded by men who are better educated, trained in new techniques with which the priest is generally not familiar. It may well be that this is a step forward for the priest, who is now freed from many social roles which had served to obscure his true priestly mission. However, it leaves the priest the task of creating the conditions of his own acceptance within the Christian community and the whole of society.

The automatic acceptance he received in older, static so- cieties will no longer be there to make his social status for him. A continuing effort and striving will be required of him if he is to achieve his own identity and function, and make this meaningful to men around him. This is neatly stated by Erikson: "Status expresses a different relativity in a more mobile society; it resembles an escalator more than a platform; it is a vehicle rather than a goal."[3]

This achievement of identity and role can be done only through the totality of the priest's dedication to the priest- hood itself, and by the constant effort to make his priesthood credible and meaningful to himself as well as to the other men of his time. He must be showing, in the way of his living, the ideal of Christ serving the Church in the libera- tion of love; but for this to be seen, the priest himself must be aiming also at the human ideal of today. Men must be able to see the human as well as the divine in the person of the priest.

It is in the wide framework of this sociological evolution that we have tried to consider the priest's own life-dedication in celibacy. In a time of rapid social change there is a con-

[3] Erik H. Erikson, *Childhood and Society*, New York: W. W. Norton, 1950, p. 246.

stant danger that the priest will be left behind, speaking from a position of yesterday to men who have passed him by. We have all, at times, seen the example of a priest who tries to act out in California the idealized social role of the pastor of his boyhood in Europe fifty years ago. What may not be so evident is the way in which all of us must not only be fully priests, but also genuinely men of our own time and place.

The discussion which, it is hoped, this book might help to spark, may well center round the dynamics of love, freedom, and law as they are actually experienced in human beings. It is clear, in the abstract, that law does not restrict true freedom but is a framework upholding it, and that both have love as their aim and fulfillment. However, we often experience within us a great tension and dichotomy between law and freedom, between law and the human fulfillment of love. This is an area of great moment in psychology, and provides constant misunderstanding and controversy between the psychologist and the philosopher. We see in the work of marriage counseling the practical aspect of this question. A young couple, sincerely in love, pledge themselves to one another and are bound by the firm objective law of marriage. One of them grows up a little more through the marriage relationship, the other slips back into immature attitudes and infantile reactions. Before long, with no conscious malice on either side, there seems to be no love between them any more, and one of them is looking for freedom. It is often possible to hold such a marriage together at a lower level of kindness, sympathy, and friendliness while an attempt is made to rebuild more positive attitudes which can lead back to love.

But with a priest it is not so easy; he, too, is bound by an objective bond of law which is meant as a framework on which love may grow, as a challenge to deeper love and service. When, through some unsuspected weakness or immaturity, the high energy of his dedication seems to fail him, to mean nothing any more, can he, psychologically speaking, continue on at a lower level? If even the sacrificial aspect of love does not move his spirit to obedience, how will he keep the law of celibacy? Those who have had to advise priests in these circumstances will know that there are no easy answers. It is often said that celibacy without charity is dead. The priest knows that the love in his life is the Holy Spirit of Jesus, calling for his love in response. But this must be a real response in freedom, not a mere fiction of law. A formal legal obedience, while good in itself as a point of beginning, is not the whole answer in freely dedicated love necessary for the priest to carry out his mission in the Church.

This is the reason that some today are urging that the spontaneous freedom of the priest's self-giving should be emphasized not only in the beginning, but through the years of his priestly service. This would be a serious modification of the celibacy law, but there seems to be some growing opinion in its favor. For it is only when love is given in freedom that it produces freedom in the human spirit. One of the qualities most cherished in the sexual interchange of love in marriage is the sense of emancipation and liberation of the self. The whole process of the growth of sexuality in the child and the adolescent is a movement towards this adult liberation of the self which is bound in the fulfillment of love and joy in the other. This is felt in the deep center of the person as a new way of mature freedom. But without free self-surrender there is no liberation, nor freedom of the spirit.

If a priest's celibacy does not continue in him as a free and total self-surrender, there is no liberation of his self at any deep personal level, and he will not be free for service, not free for love; he will have nothing personal to give to men. It may seem strange to end a book on an unsolved problem, but it has been our purpose throughout to open up this question of priestly celibacy rather than to produce final solutions. It may be sufficient for the moment to open our eyes to the complex of problems that beset the life-dedication of the Catholic priests of today, to suggest some immediate lines of reform within our present customs and institutions, and to hope that more discussion may help us to understand the way of further progress.

13:

THE WINDS OF CHANGE

THE WINDS OF CHANGE are blowing today, not only in Africa, but through the wide world. Here, on these South Sea islands where I live, we feel the fresh vigor of the trade winds, these winds that drove the sails of our forefathers, Polynesian and European, across the oceans. Today's winds are bringing us news and rumors of change among men, of change in the Church. A priest who lives far away at the world's end feels keenly the isolation of being on a quiet island in the ocean; but perhaps he may have the duty of one on a high vantage point, to tell others what he sees, and what he feels is in the wind.

For the life-giving winds of our oceans are the ancient symbol of the Holy Spirit. The author of Genesis tells us that the wind of God stirred over the waters of the first creation, giving to us of a later time a beautiful symbol of the creative love of the Spirit. In the new creation of Pentecost the wind of God comes again with a great sound from heaven, to tell us of the Spirit who is to take up his dwelling in the hearts of men. And, like a breath of new life, the Spirit is ever energizing the community of God's people with his creative love, ever stirring over the affairs of men.

Reading over what I have written, I am sure that it will be open to many objections—some of these I can see for myself, many have been put strongly by my friends in discussion on this topic. The most sweeping of these may well be that I have presented a one-sided argument rather than a balanced statement, a polemic rather than a calm discussion. I can only say again that I have not tried to write a textbook or a learned thesis, with a nice balance of contrasting views. I have tried to make this book a forceful statement of the things I see, and to pose searching questions even in areas where I do not have any answers. In this kind of book, it is inevitable that I cannot give the same kind of emphasis, conviction, and space to those with whom I am not in full agreement; they have written their own books and articles. In trying to present a new synthesis, I am confident that views other than mine have already been well noted and expressed for a long time, and no doubt, will be further developed in the future.

Perhaps a more important objection would be that my approach to celibacy is too naturalistic—that I see it as merely a human problem in the area of psychology and sociology, that I neglect the supernatural dimension, and particularly the power of grace in the life of the priest. This may well be because of the way that I see the priestly consecration of today as presenting a problem. I do not think that it is basically a problem of theology. The theology of celibacy is being gradually developed and expounded by the expert theologians to whom I have referred in the text; I am sure that the theological view will be well represented in future discussion.

I would have liked to develop, much more fully than I have done, some further reasoning from the nature of the Church and from the kind of service the Church may demand of a priest in terms of total consecration to the ideals of the Cross and the Resurrection, even to the point of martyrdom. My raising of the question of the legal form of the priest's life-commitment for a changing time and circumstance, does not involve any questioning of the above ideal, nor of the value of the theological approach. It is rather that I have something to add from the viewpoint of psychology, history, and sociology that comes into focus as a question. How can these high ideals which we share be renewed and revitalized for the priests of today, living in the community of today?

For it is necessary to emphasize again, at the end, that the theological ideal of the high Christian commitment of celibacy must find its expression in a human context. Celibacy is one of the means by which the Church presents the Christian values of a creative love centering on the Spirit of Jesus, a love beyond the waiting period of time in this world, which gives an extra dimension of meaning to all the love-values of our human experience. If the priest is to present a convincing personal witness to this love in the lesson of his life, his celibacy must be, first of all, meaningful to him.

The love we are speaking of is symbolized by the Cross and the Resurrection; it is in this Paschal mystery of Christ that the priest finds the key meaning of his celibacy. It is not only in the Cross, the symbol of sacrificial death, that celibacy has meaning, but in the further symbol of Resurrection, the new life of victorious and joyful love, of love without end. The expression of this in a human life dedicated to celibacy requires, as we have seen, a high level of psychological maturity. Without this psychological development, it will happen only too often that the celibate priest, even with great good will and effort, will not be witnessing to the high Christian ideal, but to a distorted message filtered through the false self-image of his own immaturity. We have seen that in the sociological context, the priest of today must realize that his personal witnessing to the Gospel values beyond human experience and human time, is very often the only way he will make sense to a people alienated both from God and from the logic of his verbal reasoning.

A psychologist with whom I discussed this book pointed out that my viewpoint in psychology may be rather one-sided. He admitted that there was a great deal of immaturity and frustration among priests today, but queried whether this was related to celibacy. He quoted K. Horney on the neurotic character of our time, and pointed to the high levels of immaturity and anxiety among married people as well as celibates. He was inclined to relate the priests' present problems to the sociological change in the priest's status and role. He thought I should have greater emphasis on an Adlerian view of a power frustration, rather than on the Freudian view of a problem of sexuality-fulfillment. This is a weighty objection that commands my respect; the basic difference of view that separated these two theoretical psychologists cannot be treated as irrelevant. However, I think that my own construction does fit better the facts of priestly life as experienced today, and also, as far as I have been able to gauge them, the feelings that priests have about their life and its basic problems. Certainly there is no lack of frustration, immaturity, and anxiety among married people; might this not be for the same reason I suggest when I see it among priests—a basic lack of interpersonal commitment and dedication arising from immature levels of decision? Without this free decision and mature commitment there cannot be sexual fulfillment and liberation.

However we may argue about it, and argument is essential indeed, the demand made on the priest by a changing world must be faced realistically. We must be ready to open our windows wide, to feel in the wind the stir of new ideas, new social forms. The greatest change in the world during our century seems to be the new understanding of man which we have discussed. This is one of those great uprisings of thought which come only occasionally in our history. Many movements of ideas have been leading up to it over the past centuries. We are being challenged to reap the fruits of controversies, research, philosophizing, revolution, war, and suffering, that have gradually led humanity to begin to understand the value of man, of any man. We are moving fast into a new revolution to stand beside and give form to the revolution in science and technology. This new revolution is a renewed way of thinking of men, of feeling for human beings, of understanding how they might live in free community.

The dignity of a man anywhere, his integrity and his freedom, the whole dynamic of his growth from childhood into maturity—all this is showing a new meaning to life among men, a new understanding of what it might mean to be free, to be mature. It is no accident that it is in our time that men everywhere who have been oppressed for centuries by social pressures and outside domination are now demanding to be free.

It is to the men of this new freedom and hard-won dignity that the priest of the twenty-first century will bring the message of Christ. For the young man who begins his training for the priesthood in 1970 will do most of his work as a priest in the next century. He will, we hope, be bringing his message to men who are more free, more mature, more outgoing in their concern for other men, more dedicated to the high human values. If the questioning tone of this book has seemed at times blunt and forceful, it is because the question is urgent. The gap which so many observers see between the priest and his people may easily grow wider.

We have seen in the lives of many of today's priests a low level of commitment, a lack of idealism and of inner freedom. The men of tomorrow will not be listening to the frustrated men of yesterday, no matter how genuine their message. They will be looking for new men to be their servants in the ministering love of Christ, men who are mature, well-integrated, free, and totally dedicated. The task of facing this challenge of a changing time is one for every priest. That is why the priest on the far-off island who feels the winds of change breezing across the ocean must raise his voice to be heard.

BIBLIOGRAPHY

THIS IS NOT MEANT to be a list of all the books quoted in the text, much less of all the books I have read and discussed while writing this book. No writer could ever do justice to all the writers who have, over the years, helped to form his mind; to them I can only be grateful, as to the lecturers and tutors of one's youth, and to the friends, in many countries, who might find their ideas borrowed and worked over in this book.

This list is rather for the reader who might be interested in further study of some of the thought-areas covered in this book, and for others who are interested to see a list of the books which I consider provide the source and key material for this study of celibacy and maturity in the modern priest.

Bertrams, Wilhelm, *The Celibacy of the Priest,* translated by P. Byrne, Westminster, Md.: Newman Press, 1963.

Carré, A. M. (ed), *Celibacy: Success or Failure,* Cork: Mercier Press, 1960.

Demal, Willibald, *Pastoral Psychology in Practice,* Cork: Mercier Press, 1950.

Erikson, Erik H., *Childhood and Society* (rev. ill. ed.), New York: W. W. Norton, 1964.

———, *Young Man Luther,* New York: W. W. Norton, 1958.

———, *Identity and the Life Cycle,* New York: International Universities Press, 1959.

Freud, Sigmund, *An Outline of Psychoanalysis,* New York: W. W. Norton, 1949.

Gagern, Frederick von, *Difficulties in Married Life,* Glen Rock, N. J.: Paulist Press.

Gelin, Albert, *The Poor of Yahweh,* Collegeville, Minn.: The Liturgical Press, 1964.

Hildebrand, Dietrich von, *In Defense of Purity,* Baltimore: Helicon.

Horney, Karen, *The Neurotic Personality of Our Time,* New York: W. W. Norton, 1937.

————, *Our Inner Conflicts,* New York: W. W. Norton, 1945.

Hughes, Philip, *A History of the Church,* 3 vols., New York: Sheed and Ward, 1948.

Lea, Henry C., *History of Sacerdotal Celibacy in the Christian Church,* New York: Russell & Russell, Inc.

Lee, James M. and Putz, Leo J. (ed.), *Seminary Education in a Time of Change,* Notre Dame, Ind.: Fides Publishers, 1965.

Legrand, Lucien, *The Biblical Doctrine of Virginity,* New York: Sheed and Ward, 1963.

Lepp, Ignace, *The Psychology of Loving,* Baltimore: Helicon, 1964.

Oraison, Marc, *Man and Wife,* New York: Macmillan, 1962.

————, *Love or Constraint,* Glen Rock, N. J.: Paulist Press.

Saul, Leon J., *Emotional Maturity,* Philadelphia: L. J. Lippincott, 1947.

Teilhard de Chardin, Pierre, *The Divine Milieu,* New York: Harper, 1960.

Veuillot, Pierre (ed.), *The Catholic Priesthood: Papal Documents from Pius X to Pius XII,* Westminster, Md.: Newman, 1958.

INDEX

181